"Kumar integrates science, Buddhism, and therapeutic tools to create an insightful and useful guidebook for people stuck in rumination. This book can help people free themselves from brooding and live fuller, happier lives."

—Susan Nolen-Hoeksema, Ph.D., professor of psychology at Yale University

"This wise and thoughtful book addresses the deep suffering of worry and helplessness. It is written lucidly and kindly."

—Roshi Joan Halifax, Upaya Zen Center

"*The Mindful Path Through Worry and Rumination* is well-written and quite accessible. It helps us understand how our minds work, and in turn, how to work with our minds. I found it extremely helpful."

—Sharon Salzberg, author of *Lovingkindness*

D0200330

the mindful path through worry and rumination

letting go of anxious and depressive thoughts

SAMEET M. KUMAR, PH.D.

New Harbinger Publications, Inc.

Publisher's Note

Distributed in Canada by Raincoast Books

Copyright © 2009 by Sameet M. Kumar
        New Harbinger Publications, Inc.
        5674 Shattuck Avenue
        Oakland, CA 94609
        www.newharbinger.com

Quote on pages 28-29 © Sarah Harding and Thrangu Rinpoche, 2002. Reprinted from *Creation and Completion: Essential Points of Tantric Meditation* with permission from Wisdom Publications, 199 Elm Street, Somerville, MA 02144. Wisdompubs.org.

Cover design by Amy Shoup
Text design by Michele Waters-Kermes
Acquired by Catharine Sutker
Edited by Nelda Street

All Rights Reserved

Printed in the United States of America

FSC
Mixed Sources
Product group from well-managed
forests and other controlled sources

Cert no. SW-COC-002283
www.fsc.org
© 1996 Forest Stewardship Council

Library of Congress Cataloging-in-Publication Data

Kumar, Sameet M.
  The mindful path through worry and rumination : letting go of anxious and depressive thoughts / Sameet M. Kumar.
    p. cm.
  Includes bibliographical references.
  ISBN-13: 978-1-57224-687-4 (pbk. : alk. paper)
  ISBN-10: 1-57224-687-1 (pbk. : alk. paper) 1. Anxiety. 2. Worry. 3. Anxiety--Treatment. 4. Meditation--Therapeutic use. I. Title.
  BF575.A6K78 2009
  152.4'6--dc22

                        2009044374

11   10   09

10 9 8 7 6 5 4 3 2 1

First printing

First and foremost, this book is dedicated to all of the patients, clients, and readers I have met over the years who have taught me so much about human resilience, compassion, and potential. Each of your lives is indeed precious, and I am grateful for the privilege of having been present for moments of insight and awe in your lives.

This book is also dedicated to the fruits of your journey through life and to all of the joy within your capacity.

The Buddha's teaching, the *Dharma*, is as vast as the grains of sand on the seashore. Though my knowledge is limited and my practice is far from ideal, I hope that my understanding will help further your development and help you to actualize your inner potential.

Sarve mangalam—may all beings be happy!

contents

acknowledgments   vii

introduction   1

chapter 1   Rumination and Your Emotions: Thinking Your Way Into Depression, Anxiety, and Anger   5

chapter 2   The Mindful Path   25

chapter 3   The Maze of Rumination   43

chapter 4   The Perfect Illusion   59

chapter 5   Rewiring Your Brain   75

chapter 6   Being Content   91

chapter 7   Wellness Routines   107

chapter 8   Attaining Meaningful Goals   123

chapter 9   Resilience   137

chapter 10   Perfecting the Process   151

appendix   Mindfulness Resources   163

References   165

acknowledgments

I would like to thank all of my spiritual teachers, particularly His Holiness the Fourteenth Dalai Lama of Tibet, for illuminating the path to freedom. I would also like to thank Shri Das Gupta for being my first meditation teacher, Swami Nityananda, Swami Muktananda, Shree Shastriji (Guruji), Lama Norla Rinpoche, Jamgön Kongtrul Lodro, Chögyam Trungpa Rinpoche, and Glenn Mullin for the wisdom they have shared in person and from a distance.

This book wouldn't have been possible without my best friend, teacher, and editor—my wife Christina. Without your patience and support, none of this would have been possible. I thank our two shining lights, Javier Amrit and Miguel Anand, for being the cutest, smartest, and most loving little boys anywhere and for providing much needed play during the writing process.

I would like to thank Christina's and my families for helping with the hours of research, writing, and revision by babysitting, and providing delicious meals and welcome distraction.

I would also like to thank my colleagues at the Mount Sinai Comprehensive Cancer Center for teaching me skillful means and compassion, and for providing clinical coverage on the many writing days when I was away from the office.

I must give special recognition to the musicians who helped me by providing hours of inspiration and motivation. In particular, artists such as the Birds of Avalon, the Grateful Dead, the Doors, Pink Floyd, Fela Anikulapo Kuti and the Africa 70, Thievery

Corporation, Tool, and Black Sabbath helped the writing flow during difficult moments. Starbucks Coffee provided the setting, energy, and stamina for many of the chapters as well.

I would like to thank the organizers of the World Gathering on Bereavement in Vancouver, British Columbia, for allowing the power of loving-kindness to manifest in ways I hadn't thought possible. I would also like to thank MAPS for their continued support and dedication to finding creative solutions for healing the human mind.

I would also like to thank the staff of New Harbinger Publications for trusting me once more with the opportunity to spread hope and wisdom to others.

introduction

as I sit at my desk and write, our world is in peril; our global environment, economy, security, and health all seem uncertain. There's plenty to worry about and plenty of reason for anxiety, depression, and rumination. Because of all the uncertainty in our world, there's no better time to seek a more meaningful, positive way to live. History has shown that from times of great distress are sown the seeds of opportunity, promise, and renewal.

To facilitate such discovery in these distressing times, this book is here to help show you the way out of your current state of mind and into the potential of your future. This book does not ask you to ignore your problems or to become passive in the face of life's challenges. This book asks you to make meaningful, deliberate choices that will lead to your continued joy and well-being, to take control of the choices that influence how your brain and mind work, and how you feel.

whom this book is for

If your mind feels like a burden, this book is for you. *Rumination*— thinking about the same things over and over again, worrying about the future or the past, or staying up at night with your fears and anxieties to the point where you're led into periods of depression—can feel like the weight of the world on your shoulders, stifling the air you breathe and obscuring clarity of thought and action.

Despite the burden of rumination and worry, you're still capable of great things—including feeling better. The mindful path this book teaches doesn't pass judgment on you or your thoughts. Instead it offers you a different relationship with your mind and with your world. This mindful path is here to help you achieve your mind's highest potential and avoid getting dragged down by its unhelpful habits.

Furthermore, the information I share here isn't simply what seems like a good idea to me, but is based on techniques that practitioners have tested for thousands of years and that, more recently, have withstood rigorous scientific scrutiny. Although many of the ideas in this book arose from Buddhism, this book is not only for Buddhists. I use the language of Buddhism because it's what I know. That doesn't make Buddhism the best or ideal path; it only means that Buddhism is what's familiar to me.

You don't have to be a Buddhist to benefit from the wisdom of the mindful path. If you have your own religious faith, the practices I share can help you deepen your experience of prayer. If you are an atheist, nothing in this book requires you to take on religious beliefs. Anyone can benefit from a more joyful and meaningful sense of purpose in being alive. You can use what's familiar to you to help you understand the concepts in this book. Make it yours.

If such an opportunity for growth and transformation appeals to you, please keep reading this book.

how to use this book

My job as a psychotherapist and author is to make sure you don't need me. My job is to help you gain the skills and wisdom to live an independent and healthy life on your own. This book presents the skills I have seen work time and again for people from all backgrounds and walks of life—all religious beliefs, economic classes, and personal histories—with an emphasis on using these skills. Reading this book is not enough; you must put it into practice.

It's not enough to say that you practice mindfulness and then actually practice it only when it comes up in the book or whenever you feel like it. It's not enough to say that you're making healthy dietary choices because you made a healthy choice last week—or to say that you're exercising because you go for a walk once a month—without doing more. The mindful path asks you to practice these skills at a therapeutic dose. Like medicine prescribed by your doctor, these skills work only if you take them at the right times and in proper amounts.

This book is designed to help guide you to a better understanding of how your mind developed to the point where it is now, and how to change it. Most concepts are introduced twice. The first half of this book is an overview. Chapters 1 through 5 provide you with the information to help you understand your perceived problems so that the solutions make sense. You'll learn what science knows about rumination and how mindfulness is particularly useful to help change how your brain works so that you feel better.

The second half of this book, chapters 6 through 10, is designed to help you integrate your knowledge and wisdom into your everyday life, to put them into practice. Pay special attention to the "Core Practices" in each chapter, which you can use at any time to remind yourself of the mindful path. Without practice, skills are only knowledge. But knowledge is not enough for change; change requires action.

You can work hard to reduce the level of rumination and worry in your life, but then what? The first major step is to lessen the burden of distress, but there are many ways to do this. The method you choose should also help you improve your sense of wellness and well-being. The exercises and skills you learn in this book can help you create space in your life that's conducive to your becoming healthier, happier, and more compassionate than you are now. Mindfulness is a crucial step in making sure that your life's choices create the meaningful results you're hoping for. The mindful path is the process of making space for your happiness, beginning in the here and now.

Make the choice to follow the mindful path to a happier life.

rumination and your emotions: thinking your way into depression, anxiety, and anger

in this chapter, we'll look at what we know about rumination and worry, and how they affect your life.

The nature of the mind is to wander from place to place. Sometimes the places it wanders are pleasing, and give us moments of happiness and joy, but other times these places are distressing, and bring us anxiety, depression, fear, and frustration. You can use your mind to try to figure things out in order to be happier. You can engage in reflection to refine your behavior, solve problems, and make future plans. There is, however, a downside to using your mind in this way because of what it can do with these natural and sometimes helpful tendencies.

You may find that when you try to think things through or figure things out, you often seem to wind up feeling worse. You wind up feeling as if you're blaming yourself for all your problems, feeling angrier or more resentful of others, or feeling helpless and trapped by the walls built by your thought process. You may find it particularly frustrating that it seems as if happiness unfolds in new ways almost constantly for some of the people you know. But for you, happiness has often felt elusive, despite your efforts to get there.

Your mind seems to be stuck along its endless journey in a way that you can't seem to control. Not only do you feel anxious, depressed, angry, or scared about life, but also your mind seems especially inclined to think over and over again about the things that bother you. The anxious thoughts and feelings seem to feed off each other. If you've ever kept yourself awake at night uncontrollably reviewing or anticipating events, all the while working yourself into a stressful frenzy, then you're well aware of your mind's capacity to ruminate unconstructively, even destructively at times.

what is rumination?

People who study rumination for a living distinguish between two types of rumination: *reflective pondering*, which can be quite pleasant, and *brooding* (Treynor, Gonzalez, and Nolen-Hoeksema 2003). In and of itself, rumination isn't necessarily a bad thing. One of the most rewarding of our minds' abilities is the capacity to look back on the things in our lives that have given us the greatest joy, satisfaction, and pleasure, to hear ourselves silently retell the stories of our happiest moments or anticipate future sources of joy and happiness.

If we were to turn off our minds, we wouldn't be able to indulge ourselves in the most cherished of life's moments, whether they've already passed or are awaiting fruition in the future. And we also wouldn't be able to enjoy the present moment either. Life then might be free of distress, but it also wouldn't contain any joy.

There's certainly much more to rumination than simply thinking about things over and over again. Brooding, the problematic side of rumination, is reliving and reexperiencing conversations and interactions, anticipating your future, and agonizing over decisions to a degree that interferes with your ability to achieve desired goals in the manner of your choosing. Although you may spend a considerable amount of time thinking about what's on your mind, and expend a significant amount of emotional energy doing so, that investment often drains the resources that could help you live a happier life. You may feel that you're on the verge of breaking through into a solution, but an epiphany seems elusive and you frequently find yourself covering the same territory over and over again. Ultimately, you wind up thinking more about your problems than their remedies.

For many people who engage in unconstructive rumination, criticism colors most of their thoughts. You find that not only are you sensitive to others' criticism, but also you're often the harshest critic of yourself and the people around you. There may be several reasons for this, which we'll explore later, but for now, it's important to realize that you're capable of changing this.

Your mind may feel like your enemy at the moment, but in some ways, having an active mind gives you more opportunities to make it your friend. In this book, you'll learn how to use the parts of your mind that you currently find the most distressing to help you live a more joyful, fulfilling life.

what do we ruminate about?

Many people find themselves replaying comments they made to colleagues, friends, or family members. Almost always in these instances, rumination amplifies and distorts conversations in a more negative, critical light. Rather than attempt to brainstorm solutions to the perceived strain in the particular relationship, ruminators almost always find themselves swallowed up by the minute details of the conversation, almost despite themselves and their own wishes.

To add to this, you may often view your thoughts and actions in a negative context, assuming the worst possible future outcome and spending hours anticipating consequences that may not ever materialize or be rationally justified.

If these tendencies are combined, not only are you ruminating upon details, but also the details you're so focused upon are likely to be inaccurate—possibly creating more material for you to ruminate about. In addition, it's as if the more you try to think your way out of the situation, the more there is to think about and the higher the stakes feel for each possible mistake along the way.

You may often find yourself brooding over a conversation you had earlier, feeling ashamed or guilty for something you said or did, or feeling angry and anxious about what someone told you. You may sacrifice precious hours going over details that become more and more engrossing with each passing minute. Of course, though thinking about things in this way may make them seem more important, it doesn't necessarily mean that they are. You may also wind up acting in a way that connects more to what you've been ruminating about than the actual person or situation at hand. Your rumination can become your own private reality, one that other people might not understand or know about at all.

• Donna's Burden

One of my clients, Donna, was caught in this vicious cycle of negative rumination. A fifty-three-year-old woman who was recovering from a curable form of breast cancer, Donna came into a session fuming simply because one of her friends had asked her how she was feeling. In exploring Donna's anger in therapy, we learned that several days had gone by since this conversation had taken place. Because she knew her friend was aware of her cancer treatment, she felt that it was condescending to ask how she was feeling. On the other hand, because she had cancer, Donna was upset that friends didn't call more often to support her. She spent hours alone in her room, ignoring the phone's ringing, while counting off the lists of people from whom she felt estranged. She realized that her anger had taken on a life of its own, to the extent that it overrode a reasonable interpretation of a friend's use of a standard greeting to check in on her. She saw that by following this line of thinking, there was nothing her friends could do or say that could satisfy her. All of Donna's anger had been completely one-sided and futile. By identifying the mental process that had taken place, we learned that Donna was alone because her discontent toward people's casual comments made her angry, which kept well-intentioned people away.

As in Donna's case, rumination doesn't help you work through difficult or challenging experiences; rather, it usually keeps you locked in a hamster wheel of passive negativity, preventing positive, active resolution or problem solving. When this happens, you remain frozen in the past or future, unable to resolve the present moment. In addition, the amount of time spent in rumination often isn't trivial. You can sacrifice hours, days, weeks, and even years to the rumination process—precious time out of your life that you can ill afford to lose.

• Judith's Fantasy

Judith's story is an illustration of what can happen with rumination. A widow in her nineties, Judith was referred to me by her oncologist, who was treating her for cancer. Even though she had a cancer diagnosis, it wasn't her own mortality that concerned Judith. She spent many hours every night convinced that her daughter's marriage was on the verge of collapse, simply because her daughter had made a passing comment that her husband called her once a day from his office. When Judith's husband had been alive, they had worked in the same business for many years. She couldn't conceive of spending any waking moment away from her spouse. In her mind, the fact that her daughter only spoke to her husband once during his workday was clear proof that the marriage was damaged beyond repair. By the time she sought my help, Judith had already spent countless hours over the course of many weeks brooding over the imagined minutiae of her daughter's seemingly impending divorce, including possible attorney's fees and child custody issues. When I spoke with the daughter privately about her mother's concerns during one of her visits, she was surprised to hear that her healthy marriage was a source of such tremendous concern to her mother. What's important to note here is that although Judith's fears were not rooted in reality, the depression that arose from weeks of anxious rumination was all too real.

Judith's story isn't unique. Although not everyone ruminates about the same things, in many cases, the hours spent ruminating reinforce thought patterns that lead to depression and anxiety. Repeatedly feeding yourself negative assumptions about yourself, your world, and your future helps to both lay the foundation for depression and maintain its presence in your life. Living in a zone of self-blame and regret, or constant vigilance and fear of future consequences, is also incredibly stressful. It drains you of energy that you could otherwise spend nurturing more helpful skills that would lead you to a more joyous and meaningful life. Researchers (Nolen-Hoeksema 2000) theorize that ruminators are more likely than others to have depressive episodes, as well as social and other anxiety disorders. Unfortunately, not only are frequent ruminators more prone to depression and anxiety, but they're also likely to experience it more severely.

distress can start to feel normal

Perhaps because the trails of negativity in their minds are more clearly marked and frequently traveled than any positive alternatives, ruminators may eventually feel that depression and anxiety are a normal part of their lives, to the point of being unable to believe that life has alternatives for them in the form of joy, happiness, and contentment. Part of what makes rumination so difficult to treat is that not only do you experience depression and anxiety more often and more severely than other people, but you may even also inadvertently seek out and focus on the depressing and anxiety-provoking aspects of your life more than everything else. This is part of the mind's natural tendency to seek stability, even if that stability is profoundly unhealthy or unhappy.

Imagine being able to interact with people in a way that allows them to make spontaneous comments to you and that allows you to make spontaneous comments to them. Imagine that such interactions begin and end in the present moment and that you walk away feeling confident about what happened. Imagine that you spend very little time internally criticizing your behavior toward others, that you don't use your mind to beat yourself up. Imagine that being with people is an occasion of effortless joy. With the help of this book, you can find a new stability that's much more enjoyable than what you've become used to.

trauma is something else

If what you ruminate about is a traumatic event that happened a long time ago, such as a car accident, military combat, a physical or sexual assault, or seeing someone else get badly injured or killed, then you might have post-traumatic stress. In that case, though this book might help you very much, reading it shouldn't be all that you do. Also seek the help of a mental health practitioner experienced in treating *post-traumatic stress disorder*, or *PTSD*. You may need medication and additional therapy to help cope with the trauma of what you've lived through.

who ruminates?

As you read through what happens during rumination and what characterizes people who suffer from rumination, you may find yourself feeling helpless, frustrated, or angry. You may feel as if the deck is stacked against you, that there's nothing you can do to change your history or your future. But this is far from the truth. My intention in presenting the typical characteristics of rumination and ruminators is not to make you feel helpless but to help you gain an understanding of what we know about the ruminative mind and its potential consequences on your well-being. The intention is also not to box you into a checklist or category but to let you know that you're not alone in your suffering. There's a map of what ails you, which is why we don't have to start from scratch to figure out what will help.

Keep in mind, also, that these are broad characteristics. There are no hard-and-fast rules that dictate that you fit into what the research has found or what other people experience. Every person is unique. Your history and your mind are part of what makes you unique; there's no one else like you, and there never will be. Similarly, some of the examples I give may resonate with you, but you may find that you can't relate to the specific instances I describe. That's okay; even if you can't identify with people's specific experiences, try to see if you can identify with their feelings. Even if the details differ greatly, perhaps you can relate to what some of the others have experienced who have the same issues you have. You may find that you have a lot in common.

characteristics of ruminators

Extensive research indicates that if you suffer from rumination, some general assumptions can be made about who you are and how you think. First and foremost, the bulk of what people ruminate about tends to be how they relate to others (Vassilopoulos 2008). By their intensity and frequency, conversations, expectations, passing comments, and inferred intentions can dominate your thoughts about how you relate to others. You probably think hard and often about the moments in your day when you have to deal with other people.

In addition, when you think about how you get along with other people, you're more likely to focus on the negative or stressful parts of your interactions, even to the point where you may miss positive ones (Lyubomirsky and Nolen-Hoeksema 1995). Ruminating about your role in relationships can often amplify your perception of the part you play and the negative feelings others have against you. Ruminating also often amplifies your sense of how much and how often people think about you, generally in a negative light. This negative self-importance makes you the center of attention in your own mind but doesn't make you happier.

As a result, you may even have convinced yourself that there's no part of social situations other than the negative parts, to the point where you find ways to avoid being with other people out of fear of what might happen—and especially of what could go wrong. You may be more sensitive to the anxiety of being with others than aware of the happiness or relaxation that friends and family can bring. This pattern may have persisted for such a long time that you feel as if you're difficult to get along with, love, or befriend. Not only do you find social situations stressful, but you're also frequently critical of your own contribution to any given social interaction and capacity to get along well with others. For many people, social interactions and social anxiety are so intertwined that they become indistinguishable.

If you identify as a ruminator, chances are higher that you are female (Nolen-Hoeksema, Larson, and Grayson 1999). The research on rumination has been consistent in finding that women tend to ruminate more than men. It is generally accepted that twice as many women as men suffer from rumination, and the content of rumination tends to be about relationships (ibid.). Researchers have different ideas about why women tend to ruminate more than men. There may be biological differences that make it easier for women to ruminate, but enough men also ruminate to make a biological explanation insufficient on its own. It might be that societies tend to place a greater burden on women than men to be sociable; for this reason, women may feel a greater amount of pressure than men connected to social situations. Greater cultural expectations toward women to be social can create stressful expectations that can mean that many women dissect and ruminate on their social interactions in excruciating detail.

Following this line of reasoning, if you're part of the roughly one third of problem ruminators who are male, your particular background, circumstances, or personality have given social interactions great importance for you as well, also in a way that makes you dissatisfied and often anxious. You might be able to distract yourself from stress but find that the stress of social interaction keeps coming back. You are actually at a greater risk of being isolated than women who ruminate, since men's brains seem to have a greater tendency toward isolating than women's brains do. You may be introverted as well, and feel as if you don't quite fit in with other men you know. This feeling may have been a part of your life for a very long time, perhaps even since elementary school.

Recent research, which we'll discuss in detail later in the book, indicates that the pattern of how you relate to your parents at a very young age, perhaps even in the womb, may have a tremendous influence on how you relate to others for the rest of your life (Waters et al. 2000). Don't be discouraged though; this same school of thought also finds that these patterns aren't written in stone. Your patterns of connecting to others can change, and the skills you'll learn in this book can help you change them. Nevertheless, if you have a problem with rumination, you've likely had parents with whom you didn't get along with as well as you would've liked. In fact, your parents probably had a complicated relationship with their parents as well. But remember, even though this lineage of difficult parent-child relationships may stretch back for generations, it is malleable and can be reshaped. Even though you can't change your past, you can change the direction your future takes.

Rumination research also indicates that you've likely been depressed in the past, had a panic attack, or been sickly (Cox et al. 2001). In fact, you may be reading this book because you've felt yourself fighting against the slide into depression yet again. Having been depressed in the past usually makes it easier to get depressed in the future. Similarly, having had a panic attack in the past makes it likely that you'll have one again. However, just as with your patterns of relating to people, this tendency isn't set in stone. You're not destined to continually suffer from depression. If you suffer from it now, or have in the past, once you learn all of the skills in this book and are able to practice them on your own, research indicates that if depression and anxiety resurface in your life, they won't be as intense or stay around for as long as they did before (Teasdale et al. 2000).

For the characteristics just described—social anxiety, depressive episodes, and relapses—rumination is the common factor. All other things aside, your mind's tendency to ruminate when you're an adult is the one thing that ties every one of those qualities together. As you read about these tendencies, you may find it easy to yet again blame yourself. But this is inappropriate. Aside from whether you are male or female, all of the characteristics I described can be changed, and you can help facilitate this change by engaging in particular practices and techniques that I've seen work many times before.

Also keep in mind that it's not you or rumination itself that's the problem, but the fact that your mind tends to ruminate about negative perceptions and distressing feelings more easily than positive perceptions and feelings of contentment or joy.

working with your mind

As you reflect on the characteristics I described in the previous section, how do you feel? Do you feel tense? Are there areas of tightness or discomfort in your body, such as your jaws, stomach, chest, or back? Is there shame, sadness, pity, or anger toward yourself? Did your mind wander a lot when reading the section? Did you have to reread those pages a couple of times?

If you have a sense of what you're feeling right now, you have the capacity to change. If you have a hard time identifying your feelings right now, then you can use this book to help pinpoint your feelings in order to know how to go about steering your mind toward happiness. If you can recall an example in your own life to illustrate each of the characteristics I described previously, the things that you think about yourself that stand in the way of your happiness, then you have the capacity to monitor your mind.

The insightful mind that has learned to focus on negativity can be retrained to focus on joy instead. This inner wisdom is an indispensable skill in transforming your negative feelings into positive ones, a skill that we'll expand on together throughout this book. My intention with this book is to educate you about what's helpful and what isn't in regards to your mind's ability to ruminate, and to teach you skills that science and history demonstrate will ultimately make it much easier for you to live a happier, connected, and meaningful life. If you can one day read the previous pages and experience acceptance, even love, for yourself and your exhausted mind rather than tension and negative emotions, you'll know the tools you've acquired through this book are working.

Training the mind to engage its ability to reflect with loving-kindness and seek stability around joy rather than anxiety is a much more productive and beneficial way to interact with reality and a much more enjoyable way to live. Any solution to problem rumination or brooding must not turn off the mind, but retrain it to exert its innate capacity to nurture itself rather than fight itself into a corner. Brooding over negative events, experiences, and feelings yields negative results. To focus on the here and now and to calmly find solutions to help guide the future, all the while finding greater mental and physical health and greater compassion for yourself and others, are habits you can train your mind to engage in. This is exactly what this book can teach you how to do.

the science of change and happiness

For many years, when people looked into what causes our minds to behave as they do, we looked for a single, simple explanation. Recently, a more realistic way of looking into the mind has developed. Instead of looking for single answers that can only explain parts of things, we now look at how many different factors help patterns to emerge and then keep them locked into place. This way of looking at complex systems of interactions offers a better understanding not only of how we come to be who we are but also of what things we need to address to create lasting change.

People who study the dynamics of rumination also study the mechanisms that change it as well. Over the years, a number of different strategies have been devised and tested. At this point, we can get a realistic sense of how to successfully treat rumination. We also have a more informed understanding of how the brain, mind, and spirit interact to influence how you experience the ups and downs of your life.

Don't Think About It?

For the most part, psychological research has consistently found that trying not to think about something, called *thought suppression*, doesn't work very well on its own (Wegner et al. 1987). Thought suppression has a paradoxical relationship to rumination: the harder you try not to think about something, the harder it seems to avoid it in the long run. You can't repress the things you want to ruminate about.

Instead, what seems to work consistently better is learning to allow these thoughts to happen, and finding a different way to react to them (Broderick 2005). One particularly well-researched and successful technique involves witnessing thoughts as they arise, without feeding them, while mostly focusing your awareness on your breath. This process, called *mindfulness*, seems to consistently improve negative mental habits like rumination and the distress it so often brings.

Well-Being

Before we delve further into mindfulness, it seems helpful to get a sense of what the goal looks like. What do we know about being happy, feeling satisfied with our lives, and having a sustained sense of well-being? Fortunately, we live in a time when we can use a research-based approach to develop a sense of what can help us be happier and more satisfied with life.

Genes: Surprisingly, much of how you feel can be traced to your genes (Lyubomirsky, Sheldon, and Schkade 2005). We seem to have a set point that we navigate toward, like the temperature on a thermostat. We travel around this set point during our lives, frequently returning there after our ups and downs. If your parents were depressed or anxious, chances are your genes are primed for depression and anxiety as well. However, in the same way our understanding has grown regarding how our genes are responsible for the long-term consequences of how our brains and bodies function, we've also begun to appreciate the fact that we still have the capacity to make choices about how we act and feel. For this reason, the same science that suggests that our emotional set points may be genetic also suggests that what we do with our circumstances and the goals we set can have a tremendous influence on how our genes express these set points. Our genes don't control our minds, but our minds *can* influence how our genes work.

Goals: To change how your mind operates, you need to have a goal for it to work toward. Otherwise, you can quite easily run adrift, meandering without making meaningful progress toward living the life you want to live. To set realistic goals for how to deal with rumination, we also need to discuss happiness. Happiness is not a light switch. You can't turn it on and leave it on. It's more like a candle in the breeze. Frequently extinguished, it needs to be relit over and over again. Learning how to reignite the flame will help you over time feel happier and more sure of your ability to be happy with yourself and others.

Characteristics of Happiness

Within the fields of mind science and brain science is a sense of the prevalent characteristics among people who report the highest levels of well-being and happiness. Like people who report higher rates of depression, people who report being happier tend to have an unrealistic view of their relationships. Whereas ruminators and people prone to depression tend to see their interactions with others in a negative light, happier people tend to have built an illusionary world that helps them sustain happiness, forgive others, and want to be around people (Taylor and Brown 1994).

Just as your negative worldview might influence your life to become, or seem to be, more negative over time, the positive illusions of happy people may make them feel more successful and happy. The irony is that although depressed people have an unrealistic and inaccurate, negative view of themselves, how they see the world itself tends to be somewhat more accurate than how happier people see it (Ackermann and DeRubeis 1991). People primed for depression, then, are inaccurate when thinking about themselves but more realistic when thinking about the world; people primed for happiness are unrealistic when thinking about the world but are more accurate when thinking about themselves.

When you read words like "accurate" or "realistic," a part of you may think it possible to be 100 percent correct in how you see yourself and the world. However, very few of us ever really have totally accurate grasps on reality. What appears to happen instead is that how we view the world and ourselves is a subjective process that operates on several scales simultaneously.

We can view ourselves one way, our experiences another way, and our relationships and the world around us on yet another scale. The fact that these separate scales rely on our experience of reality rather than objective reality itself actually gives us some freedom in choosing how we feel from day to day. Your mind has more freedom in the capacity to choose how it functions than you have in almost any other part of your life. You can't choose your parents. You can't choose your body. For the most part, you certainly can't choose what direction world events take. An example that His Holiness the Dalai Lama (Gyatso 2004) uses in many of his lectures comes to mind. He discusses how cultivating mental health is more crucial for happiness than cultivating physical health, because even with physical pain, you can experience happiness. The reverse isn't true; physical comfort doesn't necessarily bring happiness. The mind is much more powerful.

In many ways, it indeed seems that happiness is a choice that doesn't always rely on your reality or the world around you. Happier people seem to experience and perceive the world in an inaccurate way to keep themselves happier than they might be expected to be. In working with hundreds of people dying from cancer, I've always been struck by the fact that the level of illness, pain, and suffering sometimes has nothing to do with the feelings of patients and their families. They may be dealing with incredibly distressing situations but choose to focus on the small grains of joy that can be found only by sifting through the painful suffering. At the end of the day, they remember these precious grains the most, almost taking their suffering for granted.

We can learn from these "happily unrealistic" people in the world. They tell us that we all live in worlds that, for the most part, are illusory. Negative illusions help us live our lives more negatively, while positive illusions help us live more positively. If you're reading this book, you can choose to be wherever you want on the continuum of happiness—perhaps somewhere halfway to "ignorant bliss." You have a decision to make, a choice in how you want to remember your days. Do you want to be happy? I think you do.

An understanding of happiness is new to modern science. However, some groups of people have studied the training of the mind for many thousands of years, and have a comprehensive understanding of what works and what doesn't in helping all of us cultivate lasting happiness and well-being. The world's spiritual traditions have long spoken of the human condition and our struggles to live fulfilled, joyous lives in the face of a sometimes cruel and indifferent world. The tradition I can speak about from experience, and which we can use scientific research to discuss, is Buddhism. Starting in the monastic communities and universities of ancient India, Buddhist monks and lay practitioners from all over the world have engaged in the lifelong process of mental transformation as a spiritual practice.

Having traveled to many countries where Buddhism is practiced by large sections of the population, having spoken with dozens of monks, and having trained with some eminent Buddhist masters,

I've never met anyone who insisted that you must become a Buddhist to engage in or benefit from Buddhist practices. Just as you don't need to have a medical degree to benefit from modern medicine, the wisdom of psychological transformation is part of the human experience. It can't be patented, and no one can claim ownership of it. Well-being is our fundamental human right.

buddhism and the mind

In discussing Buddhism, I have no intention of promoting it or presenting it as superior to other spiritual traditions. Buddhism is discussed at length simply because a tremendous amount of scientific research validates ideas and practices that have been refined in its traditions. In this book, I rely most heavily on practices that are supported by scientific studies in mostly non-Buddhist practitioners. We'll also explore the conditions under which these practices were introduced and the contexts within which they were used to give you a better understanding of the relevance they may hold in our lives today.

The Needs of the Mind

My impression is that over the centuries, many Buddhist teachers learned that the mind needs some sense of structure in order to be trained. In many ways, the mind needs to have beliefs and assumptions about its place in this world in order to try to figure out how to live well in it. We need our illusions to organize and anchor our experience of the world. Without that self-made structure to rely on, we would all find ourselves wandering aimlessly, even chaotically, toward nowhere in particular. We need a context for the journey to well-being in order to establish goals and monitor progress toward those goals. For thousands of years, positive goals have been the domain of the world's diverse religious beliefs and spiritual practices.

Buddhism developed some 2,500 years ago, when Siddhartha Gautama, a noble from the Sakya clan in South Asia, declared himself the Buddha, or "Awakened One," after a profound enlightenment experience that lasted a week. During this mystical experience, he is said to have learned the nature of life and reality itself. Upon emerging from the experience, he remained in awe for weeks, unable to speak or function. When finally queried by his former colleagues, ascetics like himself, he began a series of teachings that he continued for the rest of his life on how each of us can proceed in our own unique way on the path of enlightenment, beginning and ending with a series of techniques to train our minds.

Adjusting Your Motivation

According to the Buddha's teachings, when embarking on the quest for mental discipline, we must have the proper motivation. If we seek happiness only as an escape from distress, the happiness we find will be fleeting, since distress and suffering are a natural, ubiquitous part of all of our lives. Happiness may be a relief but not a meaningful one. As His Holiness the Dalai Lama has taught (Gyatso 2000), if we obtain enlightenment for ourselves, yet others continue to suffer, what good does our happiness bring to the world? We need to strive for more than our individual happiness, yet our own happiness does form the essential foundation for alleviating the tremendous amount of suffering and distress that's all too easy to find in our world.

A lasting happiness is one that's not only a temporary relief but also a fundamental change in our view of our life purpose and the meaning of our experience of it. We must seek to adjust the motivation for our own happiness to one of awe and reverence for our lives and those of others. To invoke mental training as a spiritual discipline means to dedicate our well-being to that of others, as a way of improving both our own lives and the lives of others.

To develop a sense of awe about our lives while in the midst of emotional or mental pain can sound unrealistic. It can sound as if we're being asked to relish the suffering. This is not the case. When the Buddha gave his first teachings, he taught that suffering is universal; that it's all around us in seemingly infinite forms. Of the four noble truths he taught, the first declared that distress, suffering, and misery are the easiest and most guaranteed experiences of living beings. Joy, happiness, and inner peace take effort; unlike suffering, they're not guaranteed. Peace and joy must be cultivated.

The Preciousness of a Human Life

Cultivating joy means really understanding that suffering and its relief are two sides of the same coin. This coin is your life, which is a gift beyond material value. In the traditional Buddhist belief, we're all susceptible to being born as a variety of living creatures, ranging from ephemeral spirits to animals to humans to celestial deities on pleasure planets. However, only human beings possess the capacity to gain enlightenment at the level of the most evolved living beings, the Buddhas. Therefore, the attainment of a single birth as a human being is rare and precious, an amazing opportunity to find the deepest happiness in the universe.

One traditional Buddhist text, the *Chiggala Sutta* (Thanissaro Bhikkhu 2007), uses a powerful metaphor to describe exactly how precious human life is. We're asked to think about a planet covered with water. There's nothing on the surface of this planet except for one metal ring the size of a life preserver, floating along by itself. The odds of being born as a human being are said to be the same as those of a blind turtle accidentally raising its head into the hole of the ring on the watery planet. It's so difficult to obtain that once you have it, you must not take it for granted but, instead, seize every opportunity it provides you to seek lasting happiness.

The Suffering of Worry and Rumination

Whether or not you relate to the previous metaphor, I think it's safe to say that every human life is unique and precious because of the possibilities it contains, and yours is included in this category. To take better care of yourself, you must appreciate how unique you are, and why that uniqueness needs to be nurtured and protected even when you face distress. All of the worry and rumination that your mind is so good at cultivating keeps you suffering twice: first, there's whatever you're worried and ruminating about and, second, the fact that your worry and rumination can so easily take on a life of their own, robbing you of the awareness of joy, well-being, and a happier life. This is the suffering that you can be trained to alleviate.

When a diamond is mined, in its rawest form, it looks like a dirty rock. Once it's polished, the diamond reflects light in the unique way that makes it a precious stone; it sparkles and shines.

Similarly, your unique life may not be as polished as you would like. The soot of a worried, burdened mind that seems to easily find stress obscures your radiance. To give it that unique sparkle and shine takes effort, not just reflection.

Training in Mental Discipline

The process of deliberately engaging your mind is one that requires training and discipline. For most of us, the idea of training our minds sounds strange. We're all taught to read, write, use the bathroom, and retain information, but we aren't taught how we can train our minds to be our friends. Our minds are like sailboats with torn sails adrift at sea, left to the mercy of the ocean currents to drift this way and that, with their passengers all the while looking for safe harbor. Without navigation, there's no way to find your destination; without an anchor, you're at the ocean's mercy in stormy weather. Mindfulness can be your anchor, and your breath your navigator, as it has been for millions of other people for thousands of years.

Traditionally, Buddhists believed that of all the forms in which a soul can incarnate, only a human life can find enlightenment. Part of this view is that it's the duty of every unique human life to seek enlightenment actively rather than wait for it to drop from the sky. Like polishing a diamond, this human task requires training, skill, and disciplined effort. Toward this end, the practice of mindfulness is a central pillar in using the gift of life for the highest good of all of us and our world.

the mindful path

mindfulness has been practiced for thousands of years by millions and millions of people to find relief from suffering and to pursue a happier, more joyful existence. Recently, mindfulness has received a tremendous amount of favorable scientific scrutiny and attention because of what it purports to be able to do. For a variety of debilitating physical and mental conditions, mindfulness seems to help people experience less distress and more joy, while helping them to sleep better.

Distress comes in many forms. Psychology mainly divides distress into three overlapping emotions: depression, anxiety, and anger. Together, this negative trio tends to color people's thoughts, feelings, and assumptions about themselves and their world. These three intertwined conditions feed off the fuel of rumination, worry, and stress. Mindfulness seems to be able to pull up this trinity by its root, by starving distress of the fuel it needs to keep it running—and driving you crazy.

the origins of mindfulness

Before we further discuss the practice of mindfulness and the scientific proof of its benefits, let's first find out exactly what it is.

When the Indian prince Siddhartha Gautama sat down at the foot of a banyan tree somewhere off to the side of a lonely jungle trail 2,500 years ago, he vowed that he would not get up until he was dead or spiritually awake. When he got up from his meditation seat as a Buddha, or "Awakened One," he looked back on it in the awe of total bliss. The Buddhist belief is that he picked a firm spot that could stand the physical rigor of his enlightenment experience. The meditation site had to be as hard as a diamond, for the enlightenment itself was like a diamond in its indestructible clarity. It was then known as the "diamond throne," a patch of dirt and roots that had been polished into the radiant seat of enlightenment.

It's interesting to note that the Buddha wasn't sure that he would find enlightenment. Like you and most everyone else, he had his doubts. He was only sure that he didn't want to continue living with his mental limitations. He had spent the previous seven years following a regimen of austerity, giving up his family and his home, starving himself for weeks, and practicing other, more esoteric forms of asceticism that together only resulted in physical weakness and more mental confusion, depression, and anxiety. For his final attempt at enlightenment, under the shade of a banyan tree, he stripped these practices down to the most basic, pure form: the calm awareness of his own breathing, or mindfulness. From this first enlightenment experience and with mindfulness meditation as the foundation for all future practices, he taught for decades a variety of other meditations, yoga practices, and other guidelines for living a spiritually fulfilling life.

The Buddha's teachings were written down after his death. While he was alive, he shunned written scripture as a temptation toward dogmatic fundamentalism. He thought the written word should never trump the direct experience of regular meditation practice. However, after he died, his monks feared that people might misunderstand or misrepresent his teachings. Buddhist texts were then assembled in a series of conferences to maintain the accuracy and authenticity of the Buddha's instructions.

The application of the Buddha's mind- and meditation-related teachings that speak to the phenomenon of rumination is our main concern in this book. Specifically, we'll focus on the practice that the Buddha taught as the most basic and universally applicable meditation: mindfulness. Like the central trunk of a banyan tree, it's the main practice from which all other meditation techniques grow. Similarly, it will act as your foundation and base camp as you journey toward greater happiness, contentment, and meaning.

mindfulness is not emptying the mind

Mindfulness is a meditation technique; it can be said that it's the most fundamental meditation technique. Though there are many different applications of mindfulness, they all have a few basic things in common. Let's distinguish mindfulness from other meditations you may have heard about or practiced. We can do so by understanding what mindfulness is *not*. Mindfulness is not emptying or clearing your mind; this is an inhuman task, in that it's against the nature of the human mind to be empty.

Think of the fact that our skulls are bowl-shaped receptacles to hold our brains. Figuratively, our minds are bowls that hold our thoughts. They aren't meant to be empty, and they're easily filled. Especially when it comes to the ruminative mind, emptying your mind of thoughts is impossible, and although doing so may sometimes sound like relief, it would be incredibly dull. Beyond that, striving for an empty mind is a goal with questionable, possibly unappealing connotations; why aim for a sterile mental wasteland when you can aim for a tranquil, balanced appreciation of all the elements of life? Therefore, instead of having an empty mind as your measure of success, make it your goal to have a calmly aware mind.

working with distractions

Most of the people to whom I've taught mindfulness had tried meditation before but gave up because they thought their minds should stop wandering, and their meditation was unable to resolve that tendency. Part of what makes mindfulness so well suited to treating rumination is that mindfulness practice actually emphasizes the fact that your mind *will* wander. That won't change. However, *where* your mind wanders, *how you react* to where it goes, and how you feel afterward *will* change. You'll be empowered to lovingly observe and direct the nature of your mind's wanderings. In that way, rather than limit yourself to not thinking or feeling anything at all, you'll be able to enjoy the best of yourself and your life.

Rather than relying heavily on visualization as its general guideline, mindfulness relies on witnessing your thoughts while returning your awareness to your breath. Some mindfulness practitioners refer to this as *bare attention*, the sense that what's happening at the moment of practice is all that's happening. There's no attempt to cover up what's going on in your mind or around you; rather, there's freedom in accepting, a freedom that takes the place of the tension that arises from wanting to change your surroundings, adjust the thermostat, scratch your itchy ear, or tell the neighbors to turn their stereo down. Allow all distractions to be witnessed; this is the essence of mindfulness practice.

When I teach mindfulness to large groups, I note at the beginning of our practice sessions that participants should expect distractions and disturbances. Typically, the moment we begin the group mindfulness practice, the sounds of construction, large crowds, or wailing sirens emerge as if on cue. When I first began my own mindfulness practice, I was annoyed by these seemingly deliberate obstacles to silence. Over the years, I've come to understand that these noisy distractions are, in fact, the fire that tempers the steely resolve of mindfulness practice. Indeed, these distractions point you to the essence of mindfulness practice; they're environmental metaphors for your own internal noise. They bring awareness to your mind, just as ice water brings awareness to your mouth, tongue, and throat as you sip it.

In many ways, these external distractions are much easier to deal with than our inner, or mental, wanderings. We can't usually control the noise of the outside world any more than we can turn off the flow of thoughts and feelings inside our heads. However, we can control how we choose to respond to both. The nineteenth-century Tibetan master from whom I've learned so much, Jamgön Kongtrul Lodro Thaye, described it this way:

Thoughts of past, present, and future are like ripples on water, never ending.

Without pursuing them, whatever the subject of concentration is,

Upon that itself, like a master craftsman spinning yarn,

Not too tight or too loose, but just right for the material,

The wise direct their watch guard of mindfulness again and again.

When somewhat used to that, mindfulness will grow stronger... (48).

Notice that Jamgön Kongtrul Lodro uses the phrase, "...somewhat used to that..." This extraordinary meditation master and spiritual teacher suggests that even in his own experience that there's no end point to the mind's wandering. I always find it heartening when advanced masters like this say that their minds still wander, no matter how long or how well they've practiced. It's simply the nature of the mind to do so; perhaps it's a law as universal as the law of gravity on earth.

Simply put, distractions will always be around in some form. You can choose to be annoyed or anxious in their presence, but they also teach you that you can't wait for your world to become peaceful to find your inner peace; they won't go away, even after decades of mindfulness practice. However, your response to them can change. Often, because you're becoming more mindful of your world, it can even feel as if your surroundings are getting more chaotic the harder you strive for peace. In beginning the process of calming your mind, you may realize how much you have to work with and how difficult the task might prove. This is an essential part of the practice: accepting the fact that you have an active human mind that can sometimes feel like a burden but is your only vehicle toward peace and happiness.

The fundamental shape of mindfulness—like the receptacles of your skull and the mind itself—can be conceived as a bowl of unconditional acceptance, allowing everything to be contained in it. In this way, the strongest ally of mindfulness is compassion. In many ways, the simple act of being with your mind when it's at its most distracted is an exercise in compassion. It's like being the master of a rambunctious puppy; you must be firm but patient, strict but loving.

instructions for mindfulness meditation

You can't wait for the perfect location, perfect meditation accessory, or perfect time of day to practice mindfulness. Not all of us are blessed with a "diamond throne" as the Buddha was, but any spot where you practice meditation can transform into a special place, even if for a moment. The easiest explanation of how to practice mindfulness is to follow your breath. If you can sit and breathe, you can practice mindfulness. That's it. All of the other instructions are to help you do so while distractions endlessly arise and fade away.

The cornerstone of mindfulness practice is the belly breath. Otherwise known as diaphragmatic breathing, this is the technique of using your belly, specifically the area around your belly button, to slowly and rhythmically guide air into your lungs. This kind of breathing is the opposite of the tight, short breaths centered in your chest that come with anxiety, depression, and, most notoriously, panic attacks.

To practice the belly breath:

1. Place one hand on your chest and one on your belly button.

2. Breathe in such a way that, with each inhale, your belly hand is pushed out, as you draw in air to fill your lungs.

3. With each exhalation, your belly is pulled in as the air flows out of your lungs. During this entire process, your chest hand should stay relatively still, moving minimally if at all. Your goal here is to learn to let your belly do the breathing.

This breathing process may take some practice, and you may find it easier to lie down to learn how to do it. However, especially in the beginning, don't practice mindfulness meditation itself while lying down; you'll probably only fall asleep, missing out on the rewards of a waking practice.

The next few guidelines for practice help you maintain the belly breath.

1. Whenever possible, maintain an erect spine. This doesn't mean tense or so straight that you're actually leaning back—the spine should be held gently erect but not too tight or too loose. Make sure your shoulders aren't tight. Let them drop. Slouching will crowd your belly, preventing your diaphragm from driving your breath.

2. Keep your head straight, with your eyes focused on a spot two to three feet directly in front of them. If your head begins to direct its gaze upward, your neck will move, tightening your shoulders and gradually arching your spine. Leaning back makes belly breathing difficult. If your head begins to cast its gaze down, your posture will turn into an uncomfortable slouching, which also prevents belly breathing. Keeping your gaze fixed helps you track your head's movement.

3. Similarly, if your eyes begin to wander, your mind's wanderings will be given a turbo boost, moving faster and faster until they've run away from your mindful awareness. As your eyes move, your mind will become reflective and anticipate stress, rather than focus on the here-and-now reality of mindfulness practice. It can be helpful to find a spot on the wall, a soothing picture, or a spot on the horizon to focus on as a visual anchor for your mind. Your eyes shouldn't be unblinking, nor should they be completely closed. You may find that having them half open is the most effective strategy. This way, you can track the movement of your eyes as well as the posture of your head.

The guidelines for aligning the head, spine, and eyes are essential. I've found over the years that keeping the various parts of the body, such as the head, spine, and eyes, as still as possible allows the mind to notice its own movements much more easily. Otherwise, the awareness of movement becomes dissipated into the body, and the meditation sessions lack the depth of mental and emotional awareness they might otherwise have.

4. Gently touch your tongue to the roof of your mouth. There should be a gap between the top and bottom rows of your teeth as narrow as the tip of your tongue. Otherwise, your jaws may grind when you experience distractions or wander through stressful emotions.

5. It helps to sit cross-legged with your knees below your hips. If your knees are above your hips, or even at the same level, your legs, lower back, and hips can get quite uncomfortable, causing you to slouch or lean back and disrupting your capacity to breathe through your belly. Be comfortable, not too tight or too loose. You don't have to sit in a full lotus position, with your feet resting on each opposite knee, but just make sure that your knees are below your hips. If you use a chair, make sure your knees aren't at the same level as your hips. A meditation cushion may help, but the most important thing is the practice. Don't put it off because you don't have the proper accessory—the mindfulness practice is about your mind, not your cushion.

6. I've also found it helpful to gently rest my hands in my lap, with my thumbs touching at their tips. You can rest one palm on top of the other. This keeps your hands occupied, making it easier to witness each itch, visit from an insect, and physical discomfort without automatically moving your hands to address them. There may be a particular sensation that you feel compelled to address. Before you scratch whatever actual or metaphorical itch you experience, try to simply be aware of the sensation. It may resolve on its own, or your mind may find a new distraction to take its place.

As you engage in the practice, your mind's attitude should be one of open welcoming. I've found it immensely helpful to count each exhalation, one at a time, in order to help anchor the mind to the breath. That is, as you exhale the first breath, you can silently count, "one." You can follow the second exhalation with a silent "two" and so on. Counting the exhalations one by one helps to draw them out longer, ultimately bringing more relaxation into your mindfulness practice. You'll lose count; this is guaranteed. You may start counting your inhalations instead of your exhalations. You may find yourself repeating the same number or, all of a sudden, find yourself at a high number that you don't recall coming to consciously. Simply start over.

Core Practice:
Mindfulness Meditation

Find a comfortable spot that's not too loud or too quiet. Have something to focus your awareness on—your breath—and something to contrast moments of mindfulness with—your thoughts and sounds in the room. Recall the basics of mindfulness meditation:

1. Belly breath

2. Straight back

3. Neck, head, and back aligned

4. Eyes directed straight ahead

5. Tongue gently touching the roof of your mouth

6. Loose jaws

7. Knees below your hips

8. Thumbs gently touching

9. Counting your exhalations, one at a time

Using these basics, spend fifteen minutes breathing. Check your posture regularly. Try not to lose count, but be patient with yourself if you do. You're *practicing*.

The Mindful Breath Booster

With regular practice, you'll be able to time each session based on the number of breaths you can count, one by one. For example, a five-minute booster session before a stressful meeting or encounter may mean counting a specific number of exhalations. Over time, you'll get a good sense of how many breaths would fill up your allotted time. You'll also notice over time that the number you can get to before losing count gets higher and higher. On days when you reach this number consistently, you can consider the practice easy. If you keep losing count or find yourself struggling to maintain the counting of your breaths, you can use this as information that your mind is stressed or unfocused. In this way, the counting of your exhalations can inform you of your increasing capacity for mindfulness, as well as the degree to which your mind is distracted during any given session.

Essentially, mindfulness practice is anchoring your mind to your belly breath, letting distractions and thoughts come and go like clouds passing through the sky or, as Jamgön Kongtrul Lodro Thaye (Harding and Thrangu Rinpoche 2002, 48) puts it, "like ripples in water."

Although most of the research on mindfulness has examined sitting meditation, you can practice mindfulness virtually anywhere. Some mindfulness exercises use everyday activities, such as eating and walking. To practice mindfulness in these ways, you'll cultivate the ability to time a specific action with each breath. For example, in doing mindful walking, you can begin to lift your right foot up as you inhale and shift your weight to your left foot, bring your right foot up as your breath pauses, and finally step down with your right foot as you exhale. Each step is timed with each breath. Before you practice mindfulness in such activities as eating and walking, it's important to have some experience with the sitting practice to gain some familiarity with being aware of how your thoughts and your breath are connected.

The Therapeutic Dose

When you have an infection, your doctor may need to treat you with antibiotics. When you're given the prescription, you notice three main things on it: the name of the medicine, the quantity you need to take, and how often you need to take it. Similarly, the medicine of mindfulness also has a therapeutic dose that has been tried, tested, and found to be the most effective.

First, the meditation practice has to be done every day. All of the research cited in this book uses some form of daily practice at a minimum. We know that this dose works. On hearing this, many people immediately say, "I don't have any more time in the day; I'm already stressed out by how busy I am!" Indeed, I felt this way myself, and often still do from time to time. When I began my daily practice, I was in a demanding graduate-school program for clinical psychology. On first considering when I could possibly squeeze in a total of thirty minutes of doing what appeared to be just sitting and breathing, I didn't think it was possible. But I decided I would try it for a few weeks to see if I could do it.

After the first week, what I immediately realized was that mindfulness was giving my mind greater focus. Although it seemed that I wasn't really doing anything productive by counting my breaths for fifteen minutes that I could have spent working, the following hours were exponentially more focused, clear, and productive. Investing fifteen minutes for mindfulness practice seemed like a bargain price for the treasure of hours of centeredness and efficiency that followed.

It's important to practice meditation twice a day for at least fifteen minutes at a time (Carmody and Baer 2008). However, fifteen minutes of meditation practice can be surprisingly challenging. For most beginners, this is almost too long. Start out small and work your way up to a fifteen-minute session. You may choose to start in five- or ten-minute increments one week, adding another five minutes the following week, and so on. Many practitioners choose to practice much longer than fifteen minutes once their endurance has increased. In the beginning, it helps to start out with several shorter sessions so you don't get discouraged or overwhelmed.

I knew about meditation for ten years before I engaged in daily practice. Once I did, however, I soon grew to appreciate the concept of the therapeutic dose. It was like the difference between looking at a postcard of the Grand Canyon and sitting on its rim breathing the clean, desert air in the grand expanse of nature and sky. Like looking at a pretty postcard, irregular practice can be pleasant, beautiful, and very relaxing. However, for mindfulness meditation to play a transformative role in your life, opening you up to sustained well-being, you need to practice daily.

If you've ever engaged in physical training or higher education, you may be familiar with this kind of discipline. For example, physical exercise requires hard work and discipline. At first, you start out small, running a half mile or lifting a small weight. Over time, these small steps lead to bigger steps. No one wakes up one morning and successfully runs a marathon without preparation; they train, often for years. Similarly, a regular mindfulness practice starts out small, and the benefits may appear slowly at first until you realize that you've become a psychological marathon runner, overcoming hardship and shortcomings to reach your goal of a happier life.

Besides having contemporary scientific support, the twice-daily practice is what has been taught traditionally in Buddhist texts. In fact, many Tibetan Buddhist meditation techniques require a sworn lifelong commitment to practice multiple times a day before you're allowed to learn the technique. After six months of regular, sustained practice, it can be said with a decent level of scientific certainty that you'll have noticed some measurable changes in how you feel, but this won't happen all at once at the six-month mark. You'll experience steady improvement and progress that can be measured after six months.

Researchers have found a number of benefits associated with this therapeutic dose (Ludwig and Kabat-Zinn 2008). As stated previously, the intensity and severity of depression can be trimmed with regular mindfulness practice, with reduced risk of future episodes as an additional benefit (Teasdale et al. 2000). There's also interesting research indicating that people who practice mindfulness tend to sleep better (Speca et al. 2000). One of the most intriguing avenues of mindfulness research shows that regular mindfulness meditation practice can have a beneficial effect on how your body works. Specifically, regular mindfulness practice can improve your immune system's ability to fight infections (Davidson et al. 2003), and reduce the degree to which chronic low-back pain interferes with your life (Kabat-Zinn 1982). There's much more; it seems as though a new headline story comes out each week, touting the benefits of mindfulness at the therapeutic dose for a host of life's problems.

what to expect

In the beginning you can expect moments of relaxation in the midst of your practice. Gradually, these moments come to you more often and feel as if they're lasting longer. They'll begin to surprise you when they arise outside of your practice. It's important to remember that in the best of cases, these moments are fleeting. They change. They come and go, like the rising and falling of your breath. However, these individual moments can be strung together, like pearls on a string, to create something precious and beautiful out of otherwise ordinary experiences.

As you do with the distractions you face in practice, you can also use your life experiences to guide your mind to mindful awareness. The therapeutic dose primes your mind and brain to witness your thoughts instead of drowning in their ensuing emotions.

There will be ups and downs in your practice. Some sessions, some weeks will be easier than others. After a few months, you'll start noticing the changes that mindfulness can bring to your life. For example, I taught mindfulness to a fifty-year-old truck driver who, two weeks into the practice, found himself laughing peacefully about the erratic driving of cars around him rather than experiencing the anger and rage that had overtaken him in the past. Driving had become stressful to him, but it was his job. With the therapeutic dose of mindfulness, he found that what had been a cue to experience stress instead became a signal to remain mindful while engaged in his everyday tasks and responsibilities.

mindfulness and compassion

Traditionally, mindfulness was taught as the essential foundation for meditation practice. However, it was also understood that mindfulness was only half of this foundation. The other essential half was compassion. For thousands of years, mindfulness and compassion have been understood to be the two wings of spiritual enlightenment and psychological freedom.

Compassion is not pity. It's not feeling sorry for someone or feeling sorry for yourself. Compassion is the act of feeling and expressing a love that's totally welcoming and accepting. Compassionate love is the kind of caring that we may observe when a loving mother soothes her mischievous toddler, or when a dog owner tries to firmly but kindly teach her rambunctious puppy not to chew up her shoes. In these kinds of situations, the initial thought may be one of irritation, stress, or reluctance to confront the situation. However, although the thought happens, it falls away and is replaced by benevolent acceptance of the situation, and by behaviors that arise from a loving acceptance. The young child is held, sung to, and soothed. The puppy is admonished but with a smile and a hug. Where seemingly negative thoughts and feelings would have dictated indifferent or even angry reactions, unconditional acceptance allows for a loving response.

This level of acceptance might be easy to muster when you're faced with infants, cute animals, or people going through obvious tragedy and suffering. The challenge of compassion is to experience it in the situations where we're conditioned to feel negative feelings like anger, anxiety, or resentment. To work on these situations, you must first gain experience in having a compassionate attitude toward yourself when your mind goes to places that trigger negative emotions.

Often, we experience negative emotions twice. At first, there's the initial feeling, and then, almost automatically, this initial feeling is surrounded by an additional feeling about the first feeling. For example, we may feel depressed and then get depressed about feeling depressed. A panic attack is characterized by anxiety about anxiety.

When feelings about feelings, called *secondary emotions*, take over, their impact is exponentially greater than that of the primary emotions that they're reacting to. Mindfulness can help clear out these secondary emotions by allowing feelings to arise, linger for a moment, and fall away, all the while witnessing and accepting their existence without adding another layer of distress over them. This is part of what's meant by linking mindfulness and compassion together—compassion comes from an accepting mind, not a mind that's dueling with itself. To help you cultivate compassion toward your own mind, it may even help you to think of your mind as a cranky infant that has thrown baby food everywhere, or a mischievous puppy that has just chewed up your favorite shoes.

radical acceptance

Radical acceptance is the type of unconditional love that mindfulness can nurture. In mindfulness the concept of radical acceptance refers to this kind of all-embracing welcoming. What's so radical about it is that it's often not the automatic or easiest response. Nothing that arises in your mind is turned away. Even your darkest, most distressing thoughts, feelings, and fantasies are welcomed into the mindfulness session with the quiet reassurance of your steady breathing. There's no tension, resistance, or judgment, only the rhythm of your belly breath rising and falling.

With your mental awareness tied to the pillar of your belly breath, all sorts of distractions—criticisms, anxieties, fears, or worries; disturbing sounds, sights, and smells; or any manner of disruption—appear and fade away. In the story of the Buddha's enlightenment, he was confronted by distractions from each of his senses and impulses, which were represented by dancing maidens that morphed into terrible armies of demons before falling away into emptiness. All he did was return his awareness to his breath while keeping his mind not too tight and not too loose, just accepting.

As with the Buddha, your mindfulness is an open, welcoming empty bowl that can witness and absorb all distractions equally. If these distractions are from your environment, you witness them as you return to counting your exhalations. If they're internal distractions arising from your ruminative mind, you also witness them as your awareness returns to counting your exhalations. There's no judging, criticizing, or scolding yourself for the sounds in the room or thoughts you have. This is the twice-daily practice of mindful, radical acceptance that can transform your experience of living.

By accepting the distractions of mindfulness practice sessions, your mind learns to tolerate itself without perpetuating its ceaseless commentary on whatever it's thinking about. By engaging in mindfulness practice, your mind has a chance to watch itself, as if on a videotape replay. Over time, the mind becomes better at catching itself in the act of contributing to your stress instead of your happiness. Gradually, at first with isolated incidents but more often as time goes on, your mind catches itself choosing happiness. Your mind doesn't learn this practice by harsh discipline and punishment but, rather, with the warm embrace of radical acceptance.

mindfulness is not always relaxing

It may seem that spending some time just breathing with acceptance would be relaxing, but often it can be quite challenging. When you initially start with sitting meditation, you may experience a host of different feelings, ranging from relaxation to near panic. This is part of the reason why a daily practice is strongly recommended. By practicing daily, you get a better and more accurate sense of your mind. Your mind isn't always pleasant, so your mindfulness practice may not always be pleasant.

If you feel that you're getting immediate, positive results, you're fortunate. Many people report a sort of "honeymoon" period, when they feel that they've had a rapid mental, emotional, and spiritual transformation. Many people also report tremendous difficulty and hardship in starting the mindfulness practice. Rest assured, however, that there will most definitely come a time when the feel of your mindfulness practice changes. Honeymoons can fade into monotony. A frustrating rut in your sessions, lasting for weeks, can spontaneously break through into joyful ease. Keep practicing, no matter what the immediate sense of reward or frustration might be. This sense will change, and as it does, your practice of mindfulness will mature. This is all part of the empty bowl of mindfulness into which all of your experiences, pleasant and unpleasant, are welcome. Your task is to look at the entire bowl, not just the good parts.

Your mind's acceptance is considered to have profound implications in the Buddhist tradition. The mind oriented toward compassion is called *bodhichitta*, or "awakening mind." According to the sixth-century Indian master Shantideva (1992), the awakening mind is like a supreme medicine or a giant tree that provides shelter to everyone equally.

The metaphors that Shantideva uses are powerful, and you can use them to motivate your practice. Imagine the gentle awareness of your mindfulness practice as a cooling shade tree in the brutal heat of your mental and spiritual suffering; or envision your mindfulness practice as a bridge away from your familiar habitat of distress to the natural homeland of inner peace.

Holding you back is your familiar, automatic reaction to stress, programmed into the human body since prehistoric times. This is the universal, biological reaction to physically flee from danger or to fight it off, no matter what your mind wants to do. This *fight-or-flight response*, as it's called, was very helpful in the days when wild animals chased us for easy meals. Our breathing became rapid and shallow, our fingers numb, as blood flowed to keep our visceral organs functioning should our limbs be bitten or torn. Few of us face this kind of threat today.

In the modern world, the wild creatures that torment us are usually our own mental creations. The fight-or-flight response may have been helpful in the distant past and, once in a while, may help us get out of physical danger, but it's not so helpful when our threats are psychological. Regular meditation practice can diminish your body's tendency to engage in the fight-or-flight response, instead teaching your body a more wholesome way to respond to stress while helping to guide you toward your goals. Of course, if you do happen to be chased by a tiger, your body will immediately know what to do! But for the most part, the radical acceptance of an awakening mind is much more helpful in guiding you out of the trap of rumination and worry.

In the next chapter, we'll explore the kinds of disturbing thoughts you may frequently have that torment you, and how mindfulness can help you dissolve this torment.

chapter 3

the maze of rumination

Understanding how mindfulness can help your body to reset its stress response is crucial. However, it's really only half of the task. The other half involves understanding how the practice of mindfulness can also help your mind. To do this, you must understand how rumination, worry, and distress fit into the way your mind works. This understanding is a crucial part of becoming happier.

You can think of rumination and worry as patterns of thinking and connecting with the world that feed off of different aspects of your daily experiences. It's as if there were powerful currents flowing through your mind. The things you ruminate about—your fears and inadequacies, doubts about relationships, current or past dreams and goals, choices you face—are like pebbles that fall into these currents and wind up being carried downstream before you can examine or work with them. To understand exactly how rumination works, you need to understand both the pattern of the currents in the stream, and what is being lost inside those currents—that is, to understand the pebbles that are carried downstream. In this chapter, we'll therefore focus on both the pebbles themselves and the currents that carry them through your mind. You'll also begin the process of understanding how to liberate yourself from these currents. First, let's understand what keeps your mind locked into its distressing habits.

the four noble truths

After the Buddha attained enlightenment under the bodhi tree, in his first sermon he explained what are called the *four noble truths*. Not exclusively Buddhist, these truths reflect some basic principles of how our minds operate and how we often wind up suffering. Briefly, as I understand them, these four truths are:

- Suffering is an integral part of all of our lives.

- Our suffering arises from our desire for control and stability in an uncontrollable and unstable world.

- There's a path to freedom from suffering.

- This path to freedom is the *eightfold noble path.*

As I mentioned before, most of my clinical work is with people who have cancer. One of the things I've come to understand over the years is that a bad event or bad news, like a cancer diagnosis, doesn't make everyone react the same way. Some people are devastated when told they have a curable, treatable cancer that in reality will be, at most, an inconvenience for a few months. Other people seem to become openhearted and laugh in the face of their suffering when told that they only have a few months to live. In many instances, the difference is in the underlying assumptions that these people have about what life is all about, and what meaning they give to events in their lives. To help you along the journey to feeling better, let's focus on exactly what the nature of suffering is, and how to cultivate a measure of freedom from suffering.

the nature of suffering

The first noble truth states that suffering is ubiquitous. Often, this is unfortunately translated as the phrase, "Life is suffering." I prefer to think of this truth as accepting the fact that most of us don't have to search for suffering. Misery is readily available; we don't even have to know where to look. It finds us. Working in a hospital setting with cancer patients certainly brings this point home with immediacy. However, thankfully our suffering isn't always as dramatic as cancer or the anguish that can accompany death and dying. Most of us experience sufferings of a more insidious nature. We feel distress at slight physical discomfort, at finding ourselves stuck in traffic, or at being unable to find our favorite food in the supermarket. Suffering only varies in intensity and context; it's always around in some form or another.

Learning about the universality of suffering can seem like a bummer. However, I don't believe that the Buddha was trying to say that we should give up trying to be happy. On the contrary, an understanding of the first noble truth that I find very empowering is the realization that our happiness is not a given—it has to be sought, and you must play an active role in finding it. Since happiness, relaxation, and well-being aren't guaranteed or easily attained, you sometimes have to work hard to establish and maintain them in your life.

Once you accept the fact that suffering is a part of all of our lives, you can then direct your energy to finding happiness. From a mindfulness perspective, rather than trying to find happiness *instead* of suffering, we find happiness *in spite* of our suffering. One of the things that I'll present to you in many ways later in this book is that suffering and happiness aren't necessarily opposites. Suffering doesn't mean an absence of happiness, and happiness doesn't mean an absence of suffering. The implications of this way of looking at things allow you to work for your happiness at the seemingly most inopportune times and in the unlikeliest of places.

Chased by Tigers

One of the most popular Buddhist stories that illustrates this truth concerns a man in a precarious situation. He's walking in a forest when, all of a sudden, he finds himself being chased by a savage, hungry tiger. Running at top speed, he falls off the edge of a cliff. By luck, he happens to grab a vine on the way down, and holds on for dear life. Unfortunately, when he looks down, he sees another tiger waiting for him at the cliff's bottom. He then sees two mice beginning to gnaw at the vine that's keeping him from falling to certain death. Not knowing what to do, he looks around and finds growing next to him the sweetest-looking, brightest ripe strawberry he has ever seen. Poised on the edge of a cliff and facing immediate death, he takes a bite and enjoys the satisfying, rich flavor in the final moment of his life.

Living in this way is radical acceptance. You come face to face with the tigers of your mind, even as they wait on either side of you. Inevitably, one of them will get you. But you have at your fingertips a fleeting moment of sweetness and joy. All you need to do is open up to the happiness that might just be at your fingertips. Like a person hanging off a cliff with danger above and below, we're all often caught between difficult situations. What I like so much about this story is that it doesn't ignore the magnitude of our problems, but reminds us that where we choose to focus the mind is often the difference between pain and enjoyment. The circumstances are the same, but the choice is ours. We can either ignore the sweet strawberry because it's merely a temporary pleasure that won't take the tigers away, or appreciate its sweetness even more because it's so fleeting. The mindful path can teach you how to appreciate each fleeting joy as precious and meaningful rather than futile or irrelevant.

In the context of relentless worry and rumination, the natural course of your mind may be one that leaves you more miserable than appreciative. Happiness and enjoyment feel fleeting, while stress and distress can feel like more stable parts of your life. You may be resentful or ashamed of your thoughts and the way you wind up feeling a lot of the time. Rather than hate your mind, lovingly accept the fact that your mind is also exhausted with the burden with which it has had to live. It has been running away from its familiar tigers and into the path of new ones. Allow it to pause in the sweet relief of loving-kindness, like tasting the sweetest strawberry in your precious last moment. Your happiness doesn't require you to ignore your problems but, instead, with the disciplined application of healthy techniques, helps you find the sweetness that can exist in the present moment in spite of your problems.

Searching for Happiness

The first noble truth is like a gate that you must go through to find happiness. Many people are surprised to hear this; the first noble truth, after all, speaks of suffering, not happiness. The first noble truth teaches us that suffering offers completely equal opportunity; the only qualification for suffering is being alive. Your suffering is unique, but you are hardly alone in the fact that you have suffering in some form every single day of your life. You no longer have to waste your mental energy trying to prove otherwise. Instead of searching for a way to get away from suffering, your task now is to search for the presence of happiness in the midst of your suffering.

The first noble truth teaches us that fighting against suffering doesn't diminish its ubiquity. Instead, searching for happiness can neutralize the toll that suffering can take on your life. Using a metaphor from the Bible, the universality of suffering acts like a rock-solid foundation upon which to build your happiness. Any happiness that doesn't acknowledge and accept the reality of suffering is built on shakier ground and can collapse into a useless heap with only the slightest sign of instability and impermanence. Happiness that takes suffering into account is like a house built to withstand the strongest tornado or hurricane.

The Need for Stability

The second noble truth states that we have an inaccurate understanding of reality, and much of our suffering arises from this misunderstanding. This isn't to say that if we're experiencing intense physical pain or being abused, it's because we have a wrong view of the world, and that we should try meditation instead of seeking help to address these issues.

I believe that what the Buddha's writings mean here is that our minds tend to want to live in a predictable, pleasurable world in which we feel in control, but the reality is that our world is very unpredictable and often uncontrollable. Every time we're reminded of our seemingly absurd predicament in the grand scheme of things, our minds tend to crave stability, self-importance, and control even more than before. According to the Buddha, the conflict between our need for stability and the laws of impermanence generates the bulk of our emotional suffering.

The less sure you are that you'll achieve your goals, satisfy your desires, or do the right thing, the more desperately your mind tries to find stability and permanence. Suffering is always there, but your mind, like that of so many others, doesn't want that foundation as its home base from which to pursue happiness. It wants happiness *now*, and in the easiest, but not always healthiest, way possible. If it can't find it or if it feels threatened, then your mind and body get stressed.

building the maze

Your mind and body undergo a fight-or-flight response. While your body's energy is being consumed by the natural stress response, your mind tries to find the most familiar terrain it knows so that it doesn't have to expend any extra energy. This terrain might be familiar settings, established patterns of behavior, or underlying assumptions about your intentions and those of other people. For people who worry and ruminate frequently, this familiar terrain is the mental pattern of rumination, which, unfortunately, only leads to more stress and, with it, a new cycle of worry and rumination. The pattern itself—what I referred to earlier as the river current—becomes the stability that your mind seeks, even though what you worry and ruminate about—the pebbles carried along by that current—might change.

Over time, this pattern carves a deep groove into your mind, making it seem as if everything winds up in the current of rumination, worry, and distress. Instead of your mindfulness generating radical acceptance with compassion, rumination seems to take over and accepts all materials it can ruminate about with stress and distress. This cycle goes on perpetually, putting up psychological walls in front of you and blocking your path to true emotional and spiritual freedom. Your rumination may even involve the belief that alleviating your suffering begins with thinking hard about the same things over and over again, and that your happiness is on the other side of that path. You may feel close to the goal at one moment and the next moment find yourself at a mental and emotional dead end. So you try again, but this problem has no solution; it's full of dead ends.

Walking through life with your mind in the maze ultimately eats away at your self-confidence. You may feel that if only you could think it through some more, you could find your way off the distressing path and onto a permanently joyful path. Sleepless nights and anxiety-ridden days may be spent on this ill-founded quest. But the path doesn't seem to get any clearer, and as obstacles abound, that annoying first noble truth seems to keep popping up around every blind corner. You seem to find yourself in the same place, thinking about the same things or in the same way again and again. So you think some more, sometimes by choice, but often uncontrollably.

You eventually become trapped in the maze of rumination. Walking down the same dead-end paths is your familiar, stable, and predictable pattern of coping with the sufferings of your daily life. Unlike the meditative path, which like a labyrinth guides you to its center, mazes are full of false leads, falsely promising paths, and eventual frustration and disappointment.

Often, what you're trying to do is knock down your walls of pain and only have joy. The four noble truths teach us that although this is a good intention, it's a mistaken view. You have to find your happiness where you are. The path of the maze gives the false promise of everlasting freedom from suffering and release into a world of perpetual happiness, free from stress and worry. The first noble truth teaches you that your happiness can't wait for that impossible moment. Your happiness must begin in the present moment.

the walls of the maze

This pattern of worry and rumination shows up in different ways in people's lives. You ruminate in anticipation of something you want to do or have to accomplish. You may ruminate as a reaction to something stressful that you experienced. You may go over conversations and interactions you've had with other people. The level of detail your mind can get into is likely to be far beyond what you would like. You may find that you ruminate about negative things so much that this negativity seems to be all too easy to see, almost to the point where sometimes it's *all* you can see. The negative, distressing parts of being with others, being yourself, or living in our troubled world may have become "home base" for your mind, the place where it always seems to wind up.

When you ruminate, you usually don't wind up feeling better. Worry and distress go hand in hand. You ruminate your way into a depressed corner of your mind from which you can't seem to extricate yourself.

Typically, you worry about your social interactions. You also ruminate and worry about work, love, and money, as well as your future and that of people around you. You may spend hours rehearsing or reexperiencing conversations in your mind. You may find yourself wondering why you said or did something instead of doing the alternative. You may ruminate about the status of your relationships and the people and things that feel like obstacles on your path to happiness. You ruminate and worry about everything being okay and everything not being okay. You ruminate and worry about problems big and small with almost equal intensity.

the stable maze

What you ruminate and worry about may change, but the fact is that rumination and worry are stable parts of your life. The sad truth is that worrying and ruminating usually doesn't help you to have better relationships or to solve problems. In fact, there's every indication that worry and rumination make your problems worse (Lyubomirsky and Nolen-Hoeksema 1995). All too easily, all the worry and rumination you've invested and wasted precious hours in only make your problems seem bigger, even insurmountable. The actual issues that concern you get buried underneath all of your worry, anxiety, and distress about them to the point where your energy is consumed more by your feelings than what they're about.

Before you start worrying and ruminating about worrying and ruminating, let's explore whether there might be some benefit to this miserable skill that you've just about perfected. It might sound a bit strange, but the fact that you continue to worry and ruminate isn't all bad. Part of what keeps you trapped in the maze of rumination is the incredible amount of emotional energy you've invested in your happiness. Because you, like all people, have the seeds of resilience within you, you worry and ruminate in an attempt to solve problems rather than give up. Deep down inside, you're determined to do something productive and meaningful with your life and your relationships. You have tremendous energy and motivation, but it's being burned up in your mind. Let's now explore healthier ways to use your energy and motivation.

finding your way out of the maze

According to several Buddhist schools of psychology, you won't be able to escape the maze as long as you stay on its level. As long as your thoughts carry you through the maze, the walls around you are too high to see over. The easiest way to get out of the maze is to gain a perspective that allows you to see it from above.

This is exactly what mindfulness practice can allow you to do. By watching your mind with radical acceptance—allowing it to run through the maze as you return your awareness to your breath—you can begin to gain a higher perspective. By watching your mind think its way through the maze as you return your awareness to your body and breath, you begin to find your way to freedom one step, one breath, at a time. After a while, running through the maze becomes less overpowering. Watching your mind worry and ruminate becomes easier, like fast-forwarding through commercials in your favorite television program instead of sitting through them. The tendency to ruminate doesn't necessarily go away, but the amount of time and energy it consumes gradually diminishes. Your awareness is no longer on your ruminative and worrying thoughts but, instead, on the steps toward a more meaningful and happier life. Change begins with observation.

impermanence is permanent

We all seek to find a permanent, long-lasting happiness and permanent reasons for our happiness to stay. However, one of the most fundamental laws about reality is impermanence. Nothing lasts forever, not even planet Earth. Reality is constantly unfolding, shifting, and changing as all of the interconnections among all people and things in the world are constantly recalibrated. Time always moves forward and brings changes with it. Even your breath, rising and falling with a regular rhythm, is never the same. Your relationships, your goals, and your preferences for how to get to your goals change as well. Your mind is like a cloud moving through the sky that believes itself to be a mountain. The second noble truth is the awareness that we're more like clouds than mountains: we change and have the potential to grow as we change.

In my work as a psychologist, I've been able to see firsthand that our minds will go so far to crave the predictable and stable that we may even sacrifice our own health and well-being to satisfy this craving. Cycles of addiction and abusive relationships offer proof that the mind would prefer to stay in a toxic but stable environment rather than stir up the instability that even healthy change can bring. If you've ever struggled with addiction, you know the stability that can accompany a toxic habit. From the moment you wake up in the morning, you know exactly what you're going to do: satisfy your addiction, no matter the toll on your body or your relationships. Whether we're struggling with an overt addiction, such as drugs, alcohol, or gambling, or a subtler destructive pattern, such as worry, our minds are drawn to the desire for stability.

The second noble truth tells us that the stability we crave often closes off possibilities for our psychological and spiritual growth. The desire for stability keeps your mind trapped inside the maze. Although it may feel as if there's no way out, the stability of the maze provides some security with all of its familiar misery. You may ruminate about many things—conversations, plans, relationships— but the fact that you ruminate at all has become a stable element of your life. For this reason, your mind will resist changing.

Consider, for instance, the process of establishing your mindfulness routine. How easy was it to change your routine for a simple few minutes of breathing to help your mind and spirit heal? Ultimately, this resistance to change is not at all an entirely bad thing. In time, when you've generated stable, wholesome ways of being in the world, this need for stability will come to your aid. Your familiar, stable pattern will be a calmer, more mindful observation and response. The need for stability will persist, but the nature of the stability will change.

To help you understand that the mind craves stability at all costs, even at the price of happiness, let's focus for a moment on the depressed mind. One of the things that happens in depression is that the mind begins to make stable assumptions about the unstable world. Specifically, your mind starts to make negative assumptions about yourself, your world, and your future in what's known as the *cognitive triad* (Beck et al. 1987). Whether your depression is a passing mood or something that lasts for weeks, months, or even years, by feeding this cognitive triad with rumination, you deepen the path that depression carves into your mind. A deep rut gets formed in your mind, and everything travels on it. Eventually, even the most potentially rewarding or happiest of things can wind up fueling your anxiety and depression. One of the goals of living on the mindful path is to transform the most potentially anxiety-provoking and depressing things into meaningful moments.

Some of the most unlikely of circumstances can help get you there. Take, for instance, the story of one of the cancer patients I worked with, Anna. She illustrated the effects of the cognitive triad well. With a history of depression going back many years, Anna saw me for help through the process of readjusting to the world after being treated for breast cancer. Her diagnosis was made almost by accident, and her treatment required only a fairly minor surgery and a daily pill for five years. She suffered almost no side effects from this pill and luckily didn't need chemotherapy, radiation, or more radical surgical procedures. According to the best medical data, her risk of ever having a recurrence of breast cancer was nearly nonexistent. However, she couldn't seem to feel relief. Anna reported to me that despite the early detection and relatively minor treatment she underwent, she felt as if she were dying.

In exploring this issue with Anna, we realized that prior to her cancer diagnosis, she had suffered from depression and felt very down on herself. She was, by her own estimation, a worrywart and "professional ruminator." Once there was a possibility that she had cancer, she was convinced that she was going to die, and die alone, with her adult children far away. The fear of death consumed her ruminative tendencies, and it was all she could think about. This went on day and night for weeks. After her surgeon delivered the good news that she was essentially cured, she was in disbelief. She couldn't shake the feeling that the doctors had missed something.

According to her worldview, she only had bad luck, and being diagnosed with cancer only reaffirmed this. The fact that she had dodged a bullet made no sense to her. She was holding herself back from reentering the world or resuming her normal life, because she felt that to do so would be futile since she couldn't possibly be cured; good things never happened to her. The goal of Anna's psychotherapy was to dismantle her cognitive triad that assumed that only bad things would happen to her and her world, and that her future was hopeless.

One of the steps toward dissolving Anna's cognitive triad was addressing her tendency to worry and ruminate. In dismantling her thought process, which was fine-tuned to assume the worst, Anna also began to become more mindful of her thoughts and how her feelings followed them around like shadows. Anna began a regular mindfulness practice, and as months went by between our sessions, she reported that distress was a smaller and smaller part of her everyday life. She still found herself ruminating from time to time but was able to bring her mind back to the places that helped her feel happier rather than distressed. I'm pleased to report that three years after her diagnosis, Anna continues to enjoy health and, just as important, mental well-being.

the process is the goal

One of the most powerful challenges that Anna undertook was how she approached her goals. Like Anna, many people who are forced to get in touch with how precarious our lives can be decide to "stop and smell the roses." For Anna, this meant to enjoy her path toward her goals as a counterbalance to her rumination and worry about reaching the goals; to connect with life's moments rather than her thoughts about these moments.

Many people who hear about this approach—to stop and smell the roses or to pay attention to the process as much as the goal—fear they'll lose their drive if they change. They feel that being mindful and enjoying the journey means that they must also somehow lose the desire to pursue, and the ability to attain, meaningful goals. Like many people, Anna was afraid that becoming more mindful would somehow diminish her desire to achieve. However, achievement and enjoyment are not opposites. They work best together. Ask yourself: if you're driven to achieve your goals but miserable when you get there, have you really achieved what you wanted?

Aside from momentary stress relief, the process of shifting your awareness from the past and future to the present also helps you to break down the walls of the maze of rumination. Rather than invest your mental and emotional energy in the past and future, you can heighten your awareness of your more immediate surroundings. Often, we're all too far into our "comfort zone" of miserable familiarity to notice the little joys that seem to cross our paths invisibly every day. When your mind ruminates, it has left the present moment. You're either anxious about the past or worried about the future. Your mind is wandering in the maze. A sure way to bring your mind back into the present moment is to check in with your breath and your posture, and draw on the reserves you've accumulated from a regular mindfulness practice.

Step by Step

One of the most famous proponents of mindfulness meditation, Jon Kabat-Zinn (1990), illustrates this point vividly in his group meditations. He asks participants to eat raisins together. However, rather than gulp down a handful of raisins, each person takes a single raisin and eats it mindfully. It's quite incredible to notice with heightened awareness the intense texture and flavor of a simple raisin. It's about as close as you can get to eating that precious strawberry on the cliff side after running from tigers.

Most mindfulness meditation retreats use mindful walking as a way to break the monotony of sitting for lengthy periods. Compared to the way we usually walk around without thinking about it, mindful walking is almost like learning to walk for the first time. It can be quite surprising to realize how much intricate movement and coordination is involved in taking steps when you bring the immediacy of present-centered awareness to the task. You'll experience mindful walking in chapter 7, but for now, build up your sitting practice.

Freedom from the maze of rumination comes from striking a balance between focusing on your goals and being mindful of the process of attaining them. Applying mindfulness to simple, everyday activities can help train your mind to notice both. At first, you might be amazed by how much it seems you've missed.

Happiness is best experienced in the present moment, not just when dreamed about or looked back on. For much too long, your mind has distracted you from your happiness. Instead, embrace the happiness to be found in your immediate surroundings, starting with that which is most immediate: your breath.

Once you've embarked on the mindful path, your daily practice forms each step along the way. By cultivating awareness of how your thoughts and breath are connected, you can use your breathing to bring your mind back to the present moment. When you're driving somewhere, riding a train or bus, or walking, or whenever you notice your mind trapped in the maze of rumination, all you need to do is draw a belly breath and be aware of the sensation of air moving in and out of your body. Anchor your thoughts to your breath, and your awareness will shift to the present moment.

You can invert the struggle for control of your mind. Instead of allowing rumination to distract you, allow mindfulness to distract you from the maze of rumination that has trapped your mind for so long. There are many ways to do this, but time after time I've found that the most reliable way is to focus on your body's physical sensations. Feel the rising and falling of your breath within your body. Is it a belly breath? Is your breath loose and free? Is it tight and constricted? Is the air cool or hot as it enters your nostrils? What does it feel like to flush the stale air out of your body and fill your lungs deeply with fresh air?

Focusing on the breath in moments of rumination, worry, and distress can often be the boost that your mind needs to free itself from the miserable stability that you've grown all too accustomed to. In the midst of a cycle of rumination, connecting with the breath can reconnect you to the relaxation of mindfulness meditation practice, which is yet another reason to establish and maintain the therapeutic dose, fifteen to twenty minutes, twice a day. Falling back into the maze of rumination typically depletes your emotional resources. The regular practice of mindfulness replenishes your emotional "account balance" so that when you need emotional resources the most, you have sufficient "funds" available to see you through the difficult times as they arise.

Core Practice:
Focusing on Distractions

Spend five minutes on this exercise.

1. Check in with your posture. Take three deep breaths and settle into the awareness of your mind.

2. Does a pleasant feeling or a moment of the relaxation that meditation can bring arise? You may find yourself wishing that it would last a long time. Observe the feeling.

3. Do other things come into your awareness, perhaps the ringing of the phone, some noise somebody makes, or an unpleasant memory or worry about the future? Do distractions take your mind away from that wonderful moment in which you felt so relaxed, making it easier to criticize others and yourself? Observe the process.

4. Do you feel yourself getting upset or irritable, feeling helpless and burdened by the thought that you can never seem to stay happy for long enough, or do you feel that you're incapable of meditation because you so often sink back into anxiety, worry, and depression? Observe how easily your mind can slide into judgment about itself.

5. Generate the heartfelt wish of love and acceptance of your mind.

6. Bring your awareness back to your breath. Now relax your posture and resume what you were doing.

goals and happiness

Over the years, a lot of psychological research has been conducted on how reaching our goals can affect our moods and how we think about ourselves. For the most part, this research has found that our ability to reach our goals tends to make us happier, and being unable to reach our goals is associated with distress and low self-esteem (di Paula and Campbell 2002).

The mindful path can help you reach the goal of happiness by removing the engine of rumination and worry from your distress (Kumar, Feldman, and Hayes 2008). Furthermore, being able to actively engage in and pursue goals without getting lost in them, while maintaining your mindful equilibrium, can also help you to be more mindful, happier, and less distressed (Coffey and Hartman 2008). The next chapter will help you to understand how, for many people who ruminate and worry, the tendency of perfectionism can often interfere with the ability to maintain this kind of mindful happiness.

chapter 4

the perfect illusion

One of the foundations of modern psychology is the wisdom and understanding that our thoughts form the basis of our feelings, and our feelings then drive our behaviors. Your most basic assumptions about the world can have a huge influence on your feelings and also your behaviors. How you interpret the consequences of your behaviors typically feeds back into your basic assumptions. Changing these underlying assumptions isn't easy; most of us choose the easier path of keeping our assumptions stable, even at the cost of diminishing happiness. Your thoughts, feelings, and behaviors keep each other in a stable, predictable pattern. Over time, the efficiency of this pattern can come to be valued more than the quality or desirability of its results. Remember, change requires more energy, so your mind instead craves stability to save energy. Ironically, your mind then winds up wasting energy worrying and ruminating.

perfectionism and inadequacy

For many people suffering from excessive rumination and worry, an underlying assumption of inadequacy fuels a relentless drive for perfection. While it can be considered a drive toward self-improvement, it actually feels more punishing than rewarding. Despite your achievements, you may spend a lot of time thinking about how you've failed at some task or messed up a conversation you had, or even worrying about things you haven't done yet. Ironically, this rumination only acts to fuel the stress you feel in doing things and being around people. Rather than self-correct, you're more likely to self-criticize.

The desire for perfection is a common characteristic of many people trapped in the maze of rumination (Harris, Pepper, and Maack 2008). What "perfect" actually means can be unique to a specific person or situation. For instance, you may have known someone as a student who needed to get 100 percent on every test. Anything less than that was disappointing because it wasn't good enough; it wasn't a perfect score. This may even have been you.

Aside from wanting to get perfect test scores in school, there are many ways that perfectionism can manifest itself in your life. You may find it quite easy to recall a difficult conversation or event that you wish had had a different—more perfect—outcome. Your expectations for social interactions and accomplishments may seem quite different from your standard for the perfect test score, but the checklist you go by for measuring success is probably too rigid. One of the most significant negative consequences of perfectionism is that while you're busy searching for what feels better and more perfect, you're likely to miss the good parts of something you already have in front of you.

Perfection doesn't simply mean flawlessness. It may also mean having a narrow definition of what's meaningful or acceptable, and measuring worth using very specific standards. Your self-worth, how you regard others' worth, your relationships, and your goals all depend on whether your expectations are met and, if so, if they're met in just the right way. The price you pay for this rigid specificity is missed opportunities to find happiness, as well as other ways of defining happiness, often in the accomplishments, relationships, and goals that are already a part of your life.

the perfect fool

In south and central Asia, popular stories abound about a wandering teacher named Mullah Nasruddin. One such story recounts how one night, a neighbor of Nasruddin found him down the street, gazing at the ground underneath a street lamp.

"What are you doing, Nasruddin?" asked the neighbor.

"I dropped my keys in front of my house, so I am looking for them here," replied Nasruddin.

"But if you dropped your keys in front of your house, why are you looking for them here?" asked his puzzled neighbor.

"It was dark in front of my house, so I decided to look for them over here, where there's light," was his reply.

Like Nasruddin, we don't often look for happiness where we need to. It feels as if we have to go to some better place, a more illuminated or easier spot, before life gives us permission to be happy. But this is not the case; you have to search for happiness where it is, in the darkness, where it's often harder to find. Nasruddin could spend hours under the street lamp, but just because it's easier to see there doesn't mean he'll find his keys. Likewise, you may tell yourself, "If only such and such happened, *then* I'd be happy," or "Once this problem goes away, I'll be happier." Our society tends to encourage us to even tell ourselves, "If only I could own this, then I'd be happier."

using distractions to guide your practice

On the mindful path, happiness is unconditional. There's no need to wait for just the right conditions or look for the street lamps. Happiness begins in each moment, right where you're sitting, standing, walking, or lying down. Mindfulness practice teaches you the sometimes difficult lesson that every moment can be much happier once you let go into the potential that each moment can bring. What are you letting go of? You're letting go of the years of unhealthy rigidity that have trained you how to establish more conditions and be less happy than you want.

~~~ *Core Practice:* ~~~
Monitoring Your Responses

I often repeat this exercise, because it's tremendously useful, and forms the cornerstone of mindfulness practice.

> When you're watching your breath and counting your exhalations, what distracts you? The phone? The noise of the city? Your neighbor or children? Thoughts in your own mind?
>
> Be present for your reactions. Are you irritated? Are you annoyed? Are you still at peace?
>
> Be particularly mindful of how you describe distractions. There's no judgment on how you do this. There's no "right answer," only observation. Are you passing judgment on sounds? People? Sensations? For instance, does your mind wish for silence and get irritated at sound?
>
> Complete this sentence whenever a sound, thought, or sensation distracts you: "I feel _____."
>
> After five minutes, resume your activities. Try to keep monitoring how you describe distractions. Remember, don't judge; just describe.

~~~~~~~~~~~~~~~~~~~~~~~~~~~~~~~~~~

perfect distractions

Using distractions to train the mind to become mindful is where I feel the magic of mindfulness really happens. In many ways, distractions bring our awareness back to mindfulness. You can realize how present you were once you realize how distracted you've become. These distractions are really the wrapping paper around the gift of mindfulness.

In many Buddhist traditions, meditation sessions are timed with the use of a bell or a drum. The sharp sound of a meditation bell releasing a single note often heightens the meditation session. In these traditions, distractions are incorporated into the practice. The result is that the mind becomes more accepting, more unconditional regarding what it welcomes, while maintaining the goal of mindfulness practice.

You may find that while you're engaged in mindfulness practice, your distractions aren't meditation bells but stressful thoughts. For example, you may spend a lot of time thinking about conversations you wish you'd conducted differently or that you're worried about having in the future. You may spend so much time ruminating about interactions in this way that talking to other people may sometimes make you anxious for no apparent or rational reason. In regretting how a conversation occurred or what was talked about, you may miss seeing the opportunity to explore the potential for happiness. The parts of the conversation that worked or were fine shrink in comparison to the so-called big and bad flaws your mind gets stuck on. This probably happens routinely in other parts of your life. Your energy is diverted when you ruminate about imperfection in areas of your life rather than savor the forms of happiness that are probably closer than you think.

Core Practice:
Out and About

Consider what happens when you're driving, riding a bus, or walking from one place to another. Think about how much time you spend lost in your thoughts, ruminating, worrying, or having silent conversations with yourself. What if you used a certain part of your routine to cue you to mindfulness? A red light, a stop sign, a crosswalk—each of these things can become bells of mindfulness, reminding you to check in with your breath and with the choice to be happy. What's in the way? Is it worth your happiness?

Red Lights, Traffic Jams, and Chores

Many of my patients, and I too, have found this exercise very helpful. I spend a considerable amount of time driving in south Florida.

When traffic is at a standstill, as it often is, I return to following my breath. When I do, I become aware of where my mind has wandered and what my body has done in the meantime. I'm almost always amazed at how hard I've been thinking about things and to what extent I've driven on "autopilot." Similarly, when I pause at a red light, I observe my breath, all the details of the scene in front of me, and the clouds moving along our tropical skies. Though this exercise takes effort to recall, it can serve as a booster session that lasts only the duration of a red light. Typically, the desire to arrive at my destination and reacting automatically to traffic flows don't bring me back to mindfulness unless I make the conscious, deliberate effort to do so. Try this exercise yourself the next time you're driving or walking on your way to work or the grocery store and have to come to a stop because of a traffic signal or other interruption. Are you present to your surroundings and the hidden, everyday beauty in them as much as you'd like to be? I'm sometimes amazed at the sight of beautiful sunsets, birds in flight, and palm trees blowing in the breeze that in other circumstances I almost missed because I was lost in my own thoughts. Our minds tend to enter rumination mode very easily as we go from one place to another and also as we carry out rote tasks.

You can use another mindfulness-based exercise when you're carrying out these repetitive or "mindless" tasks, the kind you could do while blindfolded and usually just try to finish as quickly as possible, such as washing dishes, bathing your children, raking leaves, shaving, and showering. You can apply mindful attention to almost any of these simple, everyday tasks we all usually take for granted.

Try to observe what you're experiencing with all of your senses. Take, for example, washing dishes. The next time you carry out this chore, try to notice how your body feels at all levels. You can start with the details related directly to the task at hand: What do your hands feel? Is the water cold or hot? Is the water rushing out of the faucet or splashing about in the sink? Is the dish you're cleaning still slick with grease, sticky with food, or slippery with soap? Is it already squeaky clean? Focus on the sensations of water and soap on your skin. What are the sounds and smells of dishwashing? Which of the basic senses—sight, touch, sound, smell, and taste—can you enjoy while washing dishes? You can then move to other levels of physical sensation: What's the rhythm of your breath? How's your posture?

Are you putting more weight on one foot than the other? Can you balance your weight more evenly? Are you holding your shoulders bunched up and tight? Can you relax them while continuing with your task? Are your jaws tight or loose?

You can also observe your mental perceptions and how they interact with the physical ones: If your mind wanders, what topics does it wander to? Does your breathing or posture change in response to the topic that occupies your mind? Does it change again when your mind goes back to noticing the physical sensations of the water and the dish? Through this exercise, tasks that are typically "mindless" can become opportunities to be mindful of how your body feels, of what senses the task at hand engages, of what topics your mind wanders to, of how those topics make you feel, and of how the task itself provides some form of pleasure.

~~~~~~

Exercises like the two just described can help you train your mind to get outside of the maze of rumination and focus on the here-and-now stillness that follows the flow of breath and all the basic senses of your body. These exercises also train you to find mindfulness and happiness in the midst of the most seemingly mundane situations rather than wait for ideal conditions. All too often, we're lost in our thoughts, driving constantly from one mental destination to another looking for a particular object of beauty, joy, and happiness to the point where we lose touch with the present conditions of our bodies. And often those present conditions offer a different beauty, joy, and happiness, which we can enjoy in the immediate present if we have the mental presence to do so.

how did your mind get this way?

Believe it or not, there was a time in your life when you didn't ruminate. You may find it hard to remember, but at some point you actually learned how to use your mind the way you do now. No one is born ruminating; we have to learn words first and then put language together in order to even first construct coherent thoughts. This is why very young children seem to be capable of great mindfulness while playing with clay, paint, or toys. They seem to be completely present for the task at hand, oblivious to anything but the present moment.

At some point in your life, you felt inadequate about something and generalized that feeling to define both a crucial part of who you are as a person and what you're capable of achieving. You learned to equate the attainment of high standards—the high standards that you've set for yourself or that have been imposed on you—as the only measure of your self-worth. If these particular high standards are attained, then all is well with you, if only for a moment. If you "fail" to achieve perfection, then a torrent of self-deprecation, criticism, and anxiety is unleashed in your mind that carries you back to the maze of rumination, worry, and distress. You may set your high standards in an attempt to silence this torrent, but instead it's this torrent that has become the voice of your mind. Your fear of inadequacy is the force behind your quest for the perfect and meaningful moment. While engaged in that quest, you miss many other ways to assess your self-worth and many other ways to create meaning and attain satisfaction.

the perfect meal

In my practice of psychotherapy with people who are undergoing cancer treatment, I'm often struck by the ability of patients going through the worst times of their lives to find the silver lining in months of grueling surgery, chemotherapy, and radiation. It's an incredibly humbling experience to sit across the room from people who look healthy when we first meet, and week after week, watch them become sicker and lose their hair and energy level, and yet hear them say they've found incredible moments and powerful feelings in the midst of their experience that they hope never to forget. For many of these people who are fighting cancer, there's an intense sense of presence to everyday activities that they never felt in touch with before. In sickness, they're able, often for the first time in their lives, to feel the fullness of their experiences in relationships and everyday activities, a full awareness they hadn't experienced when healthy. In short, for many people, an illness provides a crash course in mindfulness.

Henry

Henry exemplifies this journey. A forty-two-year-old married father of a twelve-year-old boy when I met him, he recently had been diagnosed with head and neck cancer and had to have surgery, chemotherapy, and radiation. Because his treatment would temporarily damage his esophagus, he had to have a feeding tube put into his stomach since he would be unable to swallow for many months. Having learned mindfulness meditation before, Henry began a daily practice to help him cope with his treatment. In Henry's mind, he had no choice but to find the best and most positive path through the hard road that life had put before him against his wishes.

For all of his forty-two years of life, Henry had enjoyed eating high-quality food, and he liked to cook for his family. He was Japanese American and had a treasure trove of traditional family recipes. Unfortunately though, for Henry, cooking was quite stressful; he was a good cook but, in his words, "only as good as the recipe." If a dinner didn't come out perfectly, Henry was irritable for the rest of the night. His wife therefore also found Henry's cooking to be a stressful experience in their home. It was almost as if their time together was also only as good as the recipe that Henry followed and the level of perfection he could achieve in putting the meal together. The "perfect meal" was the hinge upon which Henry's piece of mind in the evenings turned, and it took a toll on the quality of his family life.

During his treatment, Henry tried to continue cooking as much as possible but was unable to eat. A flavorless, thick liquid that was injected into his feeding tube around mealtimes provided his nutrition. Shortly after he completed his radiation and chemotherapy, Henry shared a remarkable experience with me. While cooking, he noticed that his sense of smell had become incredibly sensitive, but not in the way that many people undergoing cancer treatment find difficult and sometimes nauseating. Instead, it was more a heightened awareness of each of the ingredients he used and a sense of how it would make his body feel. He had never experienced anything like this before. So, he did something that would have been unthinkable a couple of months before: he put his recipe book away and began to improvise. Although he couldn't eat or fully taste the food, he experienced pleasure while preparing it. For the first time in a long time, Henry could enjoy the process of cooking instead of worrying about the perfection of the outcome.

Henry continues to cook this way. Instead of experiencing cooking as a stressful test of how well he can follow a recipe, Henry now finds it to be a creative outlet. Perhaps because he wasn't allowed to eat solid food for so many months, Henry reports that he now has a new appreciation for the tastes, textures, and sensations associated with food. He has begun to eat healthier foods as well, noticing the difference in how he eats and how his body feels afterward. Perhaps most amazing, Henry reports that now he can expand this mindfulness about food sensations and preparation into other areas of his life. He has noticed that he has a greater capacity for mindfulness and a new appreciation for many different parts of life that he previously took for granted or became very stressed about. He finds that now his need for perfection in accomplishing his goals is balanced by a deeper enjoyment of what it takes to get there. The perfect meal is the one he's present for, regardless of its outcome.

happiness in the balance

It was unclear to Henry why his perfectionism manifested mainly in the kitchen. In many ways, understanding that it was there was sufficient for him to find a better and more joyful way to live without looking into how his perfectionism got there. Nonetheless, Henry did recall that perfectionism was in the air of his childhood home life. His parents, and then Henry and his siblings, assumed specific, unrelenting standards that didn't even need to be explicitly discussed. Henry and his siblings often knew what was expected of them without their parents having to explain. A mere grade of "A" wasn't good enough in his home; he had to have a perfect score.

In many homes, the demands of parents, siblings, or friends can create a foundation of conformity to rigid standards that emphasize achievement over happiness. What's missing in these environments is a balance between happiness and achievement. Working on your own perfectionism doesn't mean relinquishing your goals or standards of excellence. Choosing to lighten the burden brought on by perfectionism should never be confused with losing the drive to aim high or no longer valuing high achievement. Using Henry's example, he didn't deliberately start making bad food but, instead, found a different and more enjoyable way to prepare food and a new way to evaluate the results. In other words, he found a new sense of balance among mindfulness, happiness, and achievement that didn't exist before in his life.

The key to establishing a balance between setting goals and finding happiness is to value the journey to achievement as much as achievement itself. For most people, having healthy relationships with other people—whether family, friends, or colleagues—is a fundamental goal. Most of us derive our sense of success from our relationships and our accomplishments in the context of our relationships. We want to make others happy, and we want others to make us happy. When we feel that our relationships are going well and we're achieving our goals, we feel good about ourselves. Feeling that our relationships aren't satisfactory or that we can't reach our goals the way we'd like brings tension and stress, which makes it easy to develop a lower sense of self-worth.

your self-worth and your goals

In the best-case scenario, your feelings of success and self-worth are conditional upon your reaching your goals, goals that you're often unsure of attaining. If you succeed, you can then feel good about yourself, and all's well with the world. But the sense of accomplishment seems to go away pretty quickly. Your focus then returns to what you see as your flaws and failures rather than what you've accomplished and attained. Instead of allowing your feelings to boost your confidence and self-worth as you approach new goals, it's as if your past successes never happened and you start all over again with doubts and anxieties.

Your view of yourself is distorted to magnify your flaws. You return to the automatic thought that you're inadequate, shameful, or not perfect enough. You need to attain your goal in some specific way to prove to yourself otherwise. The satisfaction from succeeding isn't enough and is easily disrupted by someone else's casual comments or someone else's accomplishment. Your thoughts become self-critical or critical of others until your next fleeting burst of confidence. The underlying assumption—that you're a failure unless you prove otherwise—can even lead you into depression despite other successful goals and interactions.

If you don't attain your goals, then your feelings of worthlessness or incompetence grow all too easily. Feelings of inadequacy and shame may be quite familiar, since your thoughts more frequently reflect your seeming inability to do things well, rather than your skills.

The irony is that when you feel good about yourself, you're more likely to be easier for others to get along with and to attain your goals. When you feel bad about yourself, you tend to be more difficult to get along with and are less likely to attain your goals. How you feel about yourself has a lot to do with what you can achieve, and what you can achieve seems to have a lot to do with how you feel about yourself.

You may find that you have very critical thoughts about yourself. You may find that what you tell yourself and the tone with which you talk to yourself, your inner dialogue, is harsh and biting. We all have an active role to play in perpetuating our underlying assumptions about ourselves in our lives, and our minds run a commentary that constructs and validates our assumptions. The mindful path can teach you how to use your inner commentary to bring you happiness rather than the distress and tension that your mind currently brings you.

Perfectionism Isn't Perfect

All of your worry and rumination is your mind's effort to process the stress that comes from things not turning out, or potentially not turning out, exactly as you'd like. There's nothing wrong with having high standards; in a sense, perfectionism has its benefits. It's not an entirely bad thing. Clarifying the role of perfectionism in your life need not result in a lack of motivation or loss of drive to excel. Rather, it should come with an increased appreciation of balance—of enjoying the path as much as the destination. The drive to achieve and succeed can bring more happiness and satisfaction with less stress, shame, and fear.

the biased narrator

When you begin to cultivate a mindfulness practice, you find yourself listening to the commentary in your mind and becoming aware of the narrator, which is the voice in the mind we all have that speaks our thoughts and feelings to ourselves. Most of us take this voice for granted. We blindly do its bidding, sometimes mistaking the narrator for ourselves. Often, the narrator gets us to do things that are stable and familiar but that lead to our eventual unhappiness, distress, and misery. The narrator tells the story of our lives, but from a biased perspective that it has been trained to perpetuate, one that may be familiar but isn't always accurate.

A popular story in Buddhism depicts a group of blindfolded people who are asked to describe an elephant. The first person feels its trunk and states with confidence that an elephant is a long, snakelike animal. The next person feels the elephant's leg and says that the elephant is truly like a great pillar. Another person feels the elephant's body and reports that the animal is like a wall. Another, feeling its tail, states that the elephant is like a small, furry snake. They're all correct about what they feel, but wrong about what it means. The narrator in your mind is blindfolded like these people; the narrator reports what it sees as happening in your life, but it bases its ceaseless commentary on one small part of who you are—the only part that it has been trained to notice.

In my work as a psychologist, I've found that people who spend a lot of time ruminating about their fears and worries often have a harsh and critical inner narrator. The narrator uses the same tone, no matter whom it focuses on. You may be familiar with this inner voice that expresses self-criticism as effectively as it criticizes others. Not only are you capable of dwelling on your own faults, but you can also readily see the faults and imperfections of others. Just as you give your own shortcomings more energy than your accomplishments, you may also weigh the faults of others more heavily than the enjoyment or meaning of being with them.

Before you start thinking there's yet another thing wrong with you, keep in mind that we all possess this tendency to allow our inner narrators to resort to a single point of view, and to base our assumptions about ourselves, others, and our world on this perspective. The difference is that some inner narrators can direct the mind to happiness, while others perpetuate distress by reinforcing our negative thoughts with rumination and worry. The skewed inner narrator is familiar with only a small piece of the complexity of your identity. Thus, it presents a story that is partial but assumed to be complete—a story that generates stress and unhappiness. Remember, the mind craves easy answers and stability, even at the cost of your happiness. It's easier for your mind to focus on one small detail than the more complex whole; it's easier to only touch the tail of the elephant right in front of you than to walk around and feel the whole animal.

While keeping in mind the harsh narrator's presence, remember that, for the most part, "reality" is a unique story to each of us. It's essentially impossible for someone to walk around the entire elephant and touch every inch of the animal. But by touching different parts of the elephant from different perspectives, we create in our minds an illusion of what an elephant probably looks like. Similarly, we take bits of information about the world and fill in the connections among them to create a coherent concept of our world.

choosing your illusion

We all have illusions that give our world a sense of order, meaning, and purpose. Psychologists have found that people who construct positive illusions about the world, even if they're physically ill, can be happier and healthier than those who construct negative illusions (Taylor et al. 2000). In other words, if reality is like an elephant, holding the rough tail might make you feel unhappy while touching its smoother leg might be a bit more pleasant. Neither part offers a completely accurate, or even "perfect," understanding of the elephant. However, if you can only touch one part at a time, wouldn't you rather choose a part that can make you happy?

Mindfulness can help you become aware of what your inner narrator is paying attention to and how you feel as a result. Mindfulness practice can help you use your mind to find what you need to construct a positive illusion instead of pursuing the illusion of perfection or perpetuating negative illusions. By just observing the narrator without mistaking its commentary for truth, you can deliberately guide your awareness to direct your attention to the parts of your life that can help you feel more confident, competent, and joyful. Over time, by focusing on these much more pleasant parts of who you are, your underlying assumptions about yourself, others, and life itself will gradually become more positive and life affirming.

The Useless Tree

The ancient Chinese philosopher Zhuang Zhi (also known as Chuang Tzu) told a story about a carpenter and his apprentice (Palmer et al. 2006, 33–34). The two men find a massive tree that a local shrine has been built around. They keep walking. Later in the day, the apprentice asks the carpenter why he ignored such a huge tree. The carpenter replies with a harsh critique about the quality of the wood in the gnarled, knotted tree.

That night, the tree comes to the carpenter in a dream. It gently admonishes him, expressing pride in its ability to provide shade for many people and animals. The tree considers itself lucky, since unlike a fruit tree, it's not valued only for its fruit, and unlike timber, it's not considered valuable only after being cut to pieces. On the contrary, being imperfect has given the tree longevity. Before the dream is over, the tree compares its own centuries of life to the relatively brief life span of a human being: "Do you really have time to criticize trees?" The carpenter awakens from the dream with a bit more compassion and empathy, and a better understanding of what "perfection" can mean.

Attaining a present-centered, nonjudgmental perspective while actively pursuing your goals isn't something that happens quickly. Changing your illusions and ideas of "perfection" also can be difficult. This kind of change in how you live life takes time. I often tell my patients that happiness doesn't have a finish line. Happiness is a journey that doesn't stop. Reorienting yourself to pursue happiness requires discipline, effort, and practice, and, after that, constant maintenance.

Recently, many scientists have found that spiritual practices like mindfulness work in a number of ways. One of the most exciting findings recently is that mindfulness can actually change how your brain works. In the next chapter, we'll explore how you can retrain your brain to make more room for happiness to replace your all-too-familiar stress, distress, and misery.

chapter 5

rewiring your brain

"The mind" tends to be the term we use to describe the mental, psychological, or cognitive part of our experience of life. Your mind is your thinker, always communicating with you and painting your unique picture of reality. The inner narrator that we all possess is the voice that leads the chatter of our conscious thoughts. Some people view the mind as consciousness itself. Although you can observe your mind, you can't touch it or weigh it. The mind is not solid or concrete.

Unlike the mind, the brain is a solid organ, housed within the protective case of your skull. The brain is your executive organ, making all the crucial decisions that need to be made for your survival. Although it only weighs around three or four pounds, your brain requires almost a quarter of your body's energy. Your brain is always working to keep you alive. For years most scientists and scholars saw the brain and the mind as two separate, almost opposite entities. Traditionally, to study one has meant to deny the importance of the other. For example, some believe that our experience of life, our emotions, and our perceptions are all electrical and chemical processes that emerge from the complex stew of organic ingredients circulating in our brains. Our thoughts and feelings have chemical sources, and thus our experience of life is dictated solely by chemistry and can only be helped by addressing the biological basis of behavior. According to this paradigm, our minds are a by-product of chemistry.

In contrast, others believe that our experience of reality directs the flow of chemicals in the brain and that this precious organ responds to what's going on around us. In this view, our brains don't create our minds, but our minds dictate the goings-on of the brain. For people who hold this view, the mind dictates the ingredients of the chemical soup in our brains. According to this paradigm, the brain's work is a by-product of our mental experience.

A newer paradigm that I ascribe to, and the one that I use in this book, views the brain, the mind, and reality as interdependent. The brain and the mind are in constant dialogue and interaction, connecting with each other intimately and, in many ways, helping to keep each other stable—not always healthy, but stable.

Using new technology, we can track mental processes in the brain, and see changes in the brain reflected in mental changes. We're most fortunate to live in a time when scientific knowledge about the role of the brain in our lives is at a peak and can speak with some certainty about this interconnectedness among the brain, mind, and body. Now, when we talk about changing how the mind works, we can say that we're also talking about changing how the brain works. You can use the power of your mind to alter the functioning of your brain, and changing how your brain operates can help you to sustain a healthy mind.

mapping the brain

It's important to understand how the development of your mind and your brain shapes your life, and how this mental and neural development affects how you see yourself and how you relate to others. None of us is born completely ready, with all the skills we need to manage our lives. Because you are a human being, your heart was one of the first organs that began working in the earliest moments of your existence in your mother's womb. Your brain was one of the last organs to develop, and it continues to grow to this day.

It's difficult to understand how the brain develops and works. For thousands of years, two methods have typically been used. First, we see what happens when someone has a brain injury. For example, if a person has an accident that injures a spot on the brain and, all of a sudden, they start to speak differently, we can say with some certainty that the injured spot has something to do with speech. If someone has a head injury that causes different behavior, we know that the injured area probably controls the behavior in question.

The second way to learn about our brains is to study the brains of animals that are similar to human beings, which is a very controversial thing to do. First off, a lot of people question the ethics of subjecting animals to sometimes painful and often lethal experiments. Usually, the animals are killed so that their brains can be studied in detail. There's also the issue that no other animals have a brain exactly like a human brain. We may know much more about how a mouse or monkey brain works, but this understanding doesn't always translate into knowledge about human beings.

More recently, we have begun to learn about the working human brain through special machines. We can now take pictures of the brain in action. Scans such as magnetic resonance imaging (MRI) and functional magnetic resonance imaging (fMRI) can look at brain structure and function in the living brain. Positron-emission tomography (PET) scans can look at where energy in the brain is being consumed so that we can pinpoint regions that are activated by certain tasks, such as remembering happy or unhappy events, recognizing faces, matching colors, and doing some everyday tasks. The brain's surface electrical signals can be mapped out using an electroencephalogram (EEG). We can also use drugs with known mechanisms of action to see which chemicals are involved in how the brain does what it does. Sometimes these chemicals can be made into medications that can change how certain things work in your brain. All of the information presented in this book is from these more recent methods, which use the latest technology to peer inside a working human brain.

A basic assumption of any of these approaches is that the brain consumes a finite amount of energy and prioritizes how it allocates its energy. The brain in each of us operates uniquely and adapts to the skills and patterns each of us uses regularly. Like you, your brain has to choose where to spend its precious energy. Your entire brain is nourished by blood, but the parts that you use more than others work harder and require more energy. When an fMRI or PET scan highlights a pattern or region of the brain, that means that the brain is prioritizing the activities in that area over other ones. For example, you use different parts of your brain when you're eating an apple than when you're sleeping.

thinking in patterns

Let's now turn to some assumptions about how the brain works. You may recall from high-school textbooks how nineteenth-century scientists tried to map regions of the head and brain that they felt were associated with certain tasks or behaviors. These scientists, called *phrenologists*, were convinced that brain functions were localized, meaning that a particular region was in charge of something specific, like memory. Largely as a result of studying brain injury, they developed a simple understanding of how the brain operated, with a diagram that showed their understanding of what went on inside.

This was the dominant paradigm of brain science until recently. Admittedly, to a certain extent the brain does work in this way. If you remove the front part of the brain, as in a lobotomy, it's safe to say that a person's personality will become pretty flat. When surgeons have to remove brain tumors from patients, they exercise great care to ensure that minimal damage is done to surrounding areas. A small cut into a healthy brain can have drastic and terrible consequences.

However, most scientists now feel that the brain is much more complex than this model suggests. What determines our personality, behavior, and experience of the world has much more to do with the interconnectedness of different parts of the brain than merely with isolated areas. What this means is that if they look at a brain scan, they're more than likely to notice that different parts of the brain are activated simultaneously or over a short period than to notice the isolated functioning of only one spot. Scientists now look for patterns or circuits of activity.

Indeed, a lot of how you think, feel, and act can be seen in patterns of energy, blood flow, and activation that take place in different parts of your brain. We have a fairly decent understanding of how the patterns associated with different moods, tasks, and mental states look in the brain. We're even beginning to understand how these patterns were established and what keeps them stable. Each thought, feeling, and behavior has a path through your brain associated with it. Like a person finding a well-worn trail through a meadow, your brain is more likely to engage in familiar patterns rather than try new ones. The flow of energy through the brain tends to go through established paths and circuits, which is partly what makes our minds appear stable and predictable.

Certain functions, like eating, talking, and walking, are indeed associated with very stable patterns. They involve essential, deeply ingrained patterns that are almost instinctual and learned at a very young age. Other patterns are learned as your life unfolds over the years, and are in response to your unique circumstances and needs. Each one of us therefore has a unique set of familiar patterns and circuits set in our brains. One pattern isn't better than or preferable to another, just different from it.

the wiring of your brain

Pioneering neuroscientists like Dan Siegel (Siegel and Hartzell 2003) have studied how our brains develop, and how our earliest relationships affect our brains and our lives for years to come. Let's now turn to understanding how your mind developed from your brain, with a specific focus on the experiences that gave rise to the brain you have.

the earliest days

Beginning in the last trimester of pregnancy, the brain begins a period of rapid development that really doesn't peak until long after birth, in the first few years of life as a baby. Since its earliest days, the field of psychology has understood the importance of early childhood experiences and the monumental impact they can have on the rest of our lives. More recently, scientists have learned that how the brain develops during this time can lay the foundation for how we process our experiences and create the assumptions we hold about ourselves and others for many years to come. My own experience as a parent tells me that we're probably born with certain qualities, such as temperament, but our childhood experiences can determine which aspects of our personalities get expressed and how we express them.

Around a child's first birthday, several important changes are taking place all at the same time. The child is learning how to talk, walk, and self-feed. This powerful combination of milestones frees the child to explore his or her world. The child is no longer bound to the mother's side, dependent on her life-sustaining milk, her ability to carry the child around, and her efforts at understanding the child's needs and desires. The child then becomes free to begin independent play, explore the world around him or her, ask questions, and begin to make verbal demands of others.

attachment theory

How others respond to the child's new freedom appears to be profoundly important. To understand what happens around this time, two psychologists, John Bowlby (1988) and Mary Ainsworth (Ainsworth et al. 1978), pioneered what's called *attachment theory*. The primary aim of attachment theory is to understand how we relate to people, and how our experiences with caregivers in early childhood between our first and third year of life shape our minds and relationships later in life. Attachment researchers have connected how our caregivers responded to us when we first began experimenting with our freedom to how we function in relationships and our general approach toward ourselves and others. They feel that our abilities to trust others, confidently explore our world, and care for someone and be cared for in relationships can all stem from this important time in our lives. We carry with us the patterns of functioning we learned as children, and these patterns can become the framework for how our brains are wired to feel and interact with others for many years to come.

To understand what kind of relationship or attachment style mothers and their children had, Mary Ainsworth devised a simple experiment (ibid.). Called the "strange situation," it involves an observer watching behind a two-way mirror to see what happens when a mother and infant are together in a new, unfamiliar room. Someone who is a stranger to the mother and child arrives, talks briefly to the mother, and stays in the room as the mother leaves. The stranger then tries to engage the baby with a toy. The mother comes back briefly and then leaves again, returning a short time later to pick up and hold the baby. Although these experiments were done with mothers and infants, they can pertain to any main adult caregiver, such as a father or grandparent.

When the strange-situation experiment is completed, the child generally has three different reactions to the mother's return. Each of these reactions can then be identified as what's called an *attachment style*.

Secure Attachment

Some babies are happy when the mother returns, and also don't mind playing with the stranger while the mother isn't there. These children tend to feel secure in their relationship with the mother. Theorists have labeled this as *secure attachment style*, which appears to be associated with the best long-term outcomes in terms of relationships. These children are happy to explore the room, and probably feel that their needs are being met by the mother's attention. When they become adults, these securely attached children will likely seek the company of others, and tend to have the highest levels of psychological well-being (Shaver and Mikulincer 2008).

Avoidant Attachment

Other babies appear to have the same reaction to the mother, the stranger, and the unfamiliar room; they treat all three with relative indifference. They aren't too upset when the mother leaves, and may even run away from her when she comes back. At home, the mother may be disengaged from or indifferent to the baby. As adults, people with this *avoidant attachment style* may discount their need for relationships and minimize the importance of emotions and feelings in their lives. They may be out of touch with their own physical sensations, not realizing when they're stressed or worried (ibid.).

Anxious Attachment

A third group of babies can be resentful when the mother comes back. They may fear the stranger and avoid exploring the room freely. They're upset that the mother left and aren't easily soothed by her return. They may even be hostile to her when she does return. At home, these children may receive attention only when they meet certain conditions or only when they meet their parents' needs rather than their own. The parents of anxiously attached infants may have received similar treatment in their own childhoods, and are passing on what they know of parenting or caregiving. This attachment style, called *anxious attachment style*, is associated with rumination and increased distress in adulthood (ibid.).

The anxiously attached child will probably grow up to more easily remember the unpleasant aspects of interacting with others than the pleasing side of these same interactions. Even pleasant memories can make them anxious. As their social circuitry becomes established and activated, it's the path of anxiety that wakes up faster than anything else and that can color all of their memories.

Your attachment style may not have been purposefully imposed on you. Before you start blaming your mother or childhood caregivers for any emotional and relationship problems you now have, keep in mind that attachment styles, especially the anxious and avoidant types, can travel through generations (Mikulincer and Florian 1999). In other words, your attachment style may be a family heirloom that arose generations ago. It's neither helpful nor accurate to say that a parent or caregiver "gave" you an attachment style, since your caregivers may not have been aware of what they were doing.

Attachment styles aren't set in stone. If you identify with one of the attachment styles associated with less healthy development, don't worry. According to attachment theory, because you developed a certain attachment style as a child doesn't necessarily mean it's set in stone. Your attachment style can change depending on a variety of experiences; for example, divorce, illness, and death can cause an initially secure attachment style from early childhood to change into an anxious or avoidant one in adulthood (Davila and Cobb 2003). It's encouraging that positive experiences and coping styles can also transform the impact of your attachment style, buffering against the effects of an abusive or uncaring parent, or protecting you from the harmful effects of traumatic or difficult experiences (Wei, Heppner, and Mallinckrodt 2003).

The bottom line is this: Your attachment style was probably set in childhood but continues to respond and adapt to the experiences you have for the rest of your life. Attachment might be part of your "wiring," but it's not necessarily "hardwiring." You have the potential to improve how you relate to yourself and others. In a short time, you'll learn why mindfulness meditation is such an important part of meaningful change.

In the United States, most adults—about two thirds—exhibit secure attachment; about a quarter exhibit avoidant attachment; and about 11 percent have anxious attachment (Mickelson, Kessler, and Shaver 1997). Attachment styles aren't resistant to change but may, in early childhood, lay the foundation for how the child approaches relationships. The goal of healthy attachment is to establish a secure, stable base inside the mind, modeled after the nurturance you receive from your mother or caregiver. This stable base permits you to soothe yourself during new or challenging situations. When the stable base exists, it's like having the love of a caring parent acting as an inner force for encouragement, support, and hope. The secure, stable base also allows you to spend some of your emotional energy caring for others rather than become consumed by your own anxieties and distress.

how attachment styles affect adults

If the stable base—the bond between the infant and caregiver—is absent or uncaring, your mind can be hostile, indifferent, or distressing. Your mind tends to be self-absorbed or want pity, or feels as if the care you're receiving is inadequate or poor. The energy isn't there to care for others at the level you would like to be cared for. Your mind is turned inward on itself rather than outward to embrace the world, find new adventures, and explore new frontiers.

The Way Forward

It wouldn't be accurate to assign blame for how your attachment style arose. Parents and caregivers generally don't deliberately plan on being indifferent, critical, or conditional with their children. Typically, there's often very little deliberation in parenting at all. Parents usually go with what they know. Parents may try to improve on what they were given as children, but often they tend to pass on what's familiar to them. Your attachment style may also have emerged from the interaction between your temperament and your early childhood experiences with caregivers, rather than being entirely dictated by the strengths or weaknesses of the parenting you received.

Instead of solving the problems or shortcomings of your infancy, or the poor parenting you may have had or still have today, I believe it's more helpful to try to figure out how you can be happier *now*.

The Growing Brain

Let's now return to discussing your mind and your brain in the context of attachment styles. Recall that attachment styles tend to become established between the first and third year of life. This also happens to be the time of the most rapid brain growth and development. During these crucial years, you learned to eat, feed yourself, walk, talk, run, use the bathroom, and perform the basic tasks of life that you still do today. At this point in your childhood, your brain begins to form assumptions about your new world. These assumptions form the earliest patterns of your personality. The trails and circuits of brain function and brain-cell interactions get set for the first time. Throughout your life, your brain will always find it easier—but not unavoidable—to go back to these earliest patterns of operating in the world. Your experiences shape how your brain will grow (Milner, Squire, and Kandel 1998). Therefore, any plan you want to follow to be happier must also address the pathways in your brain in order to have lasting success.

balancing your brain

The brain is a complex organ that we're only beginning to understand. A thorough presentation of your brain would be much bigger than this book or any one book. For the purpose of helping you engage in the mindful path, I'll address the three necessary components of worry and rumination in your brain—the narrator, mental focus, and how your brain controls stress—and how mindfulness can change these three things.

Right Brain vs. Left Brain

The human brain looks kind of like a walnut made up of two halves or hemispheres. There has been a lot of talk recently about right-brained versus left-brained people. "Right-brained" people are supposed be more creative, intuitive, and holistic thinkers. "Left-brained" people are supposed to be more linear, logical, and rational. The insinuation in this model is that creativity comes from the right brain, and the left brain keeps us locked into a predictable and less creative way of living.

The spheres of the brain work ideally when in balance, not in competition with each other. We all have "both brains," and each side is just as important as the other. Trying to use just one side of the brain is impossible. The mindful path involves accepting the strengths of each part of your brain and using them together in the most harmonious way possible to give you a healthier mind.

The Developing Brain

Brain-hemisphere balance isn't something we're born with. In the first few years of life, the right hemisphere grows the fastest (Chiron et al. 1997). The child takes in the whole world and, since words are relatively new, doesn't structure his or her experience with language. Rather, intuitive and imaginative play is the main way in which the child interacts with the world. The right hemisphere also becomes responsible for how the infant manages stress and is deeply involved with the body's innate stress response (Schore 2001). At this time in a child's life, a connection is made between the emotional memories processed by brain regions called the *amygdalae* and other regions that are active when you see your parents or other caregivers. Called the *right prefrontal cortex (rPFC)*, these regions are in the right part of your brain, a few inches behind your forehead.

The amygdalae require some more clarification; they're two almond-shaped clusters of brain cells toward the bottom of both hemispheres of your brain. According to Schore (ibid.), they connect your sense of smell, such as the smell of your mother's milk or baby formula, to your feeling soothed. Later in life, the amygdalae process emotional memories, which means that when you remember something stressful, worrisome, or depressing, your amygdalae take part in the process that connects the feeling to the memory. Interestingly, the amygdalae are also connected to parts of your brain that are responsible for the human stress response. Meaningful memories therefore cause us to react physically. Pleasant memories can soothe us by decreasing our stress response, while unpleasant memories can trigger a heightened stress response. The same amygdalae can trigger soothing or stress, depending on what information they receive.

After around the third year of life, your left brain becomes more active than your right brain (ibid.). You begin to acquire more complex grammar, structuring your world with language and words. At around this time, during the third year, both attachment style and your inner narrative begin to become established. It may very well be that the key period of attachment ends when this inner voice becomes established and teaches us how to manage our moods internally rather than always seek our parents or caregivers.

This new inner narrator, the mental voice that tells you what you're thinking and feeling, is often directly related to your attachment style. Your inner voice begins to use words around the same time the pattern of your exploration in the world first becomes established. For example, if your main caregiver is soothing and nurturing, your inner voice may take on these adaptive and helpful qualities. The world can then feel exciting, rich, and filled with hope and opportunity. If your main caregiver is hostile, critical, or indifferent, your inner voice may take on these unhelpful qualities instead. The world can then be a fearful or anxious place, filled with danger, struggle, and conflict. In many instances, your caregiver's voice may become your own. How you learn and get along with others is now influenced by your own mind as much as the attitude of, and relationship with, your caregiver.

Our self-confidence, assumptions about how we can care for and be cared for by others, and the voice with which we talk to ourselves all seem to emerge at the same time inside our brains, consistent with the basic tenets of attachment theory. The timing of these processes suggests that from our earliest years, a link is established between how we interact with others, how we manage stress, and how we speak to ourselves. Exploration, attachment, and stress management are some of the most basic tasks of the first years of life, and equip the child with a template for what to expect from others and the world as he or she develops into adulthood. Many people feel that the signatures of various attachment styles can be found in the pattern of how the brain handles the key tasks of exploration and stress management (Siegel 2001).

rewiring your circuits

For many years, it was assumed that once your brain developed, how it functioned would remain pretty much the same throughout your adult life. However, this doesn't appear to be the case. Rather, your brain never stops learning, even as its efficiency declines with age. Although it appears that it's never too late to learn, it may become harder to do so. We now have evidence for what scientists call *neuroplasticity*, the brain's ability to change how it works and to learn new patterns of interacting with the world. The technology behind our revolutionary understanding of the brain has been applied to expanding our knowledge of emotions, attachment, and mindfulness meditation.

Norman A. S. Farb and his colleagues at the University of Toronto (2007) found that after only eight weeks of daily, forty-five-minute mindfulness meditation practice, the brains of participants showed measurable changes in fairly consistent ways. The researchers observed that the pattern of activation in the brain that's associated with the functioning of the narrator, located a few inches behind your forehead in what's called the *medial prefrontal cortex* (*mPFC*), diminished with regular practice. The brains of mindfulness practitioners seemed instead to allocate their resources to areas associated with their moment-to-moment physical awareness. These are the same regions that grow rapidly in your first years of life, your rPFC, a few inches behind your right eye. What's intriguing about this study is that after a relatively short time, mindfulness practitioners appeared to be more in touch with their experiences but not as consumed by their inner commentary. The narrator doesn't stop working but seems to get less powerful as your brain learns to direct its attention elsewhere. The narrator becomes less important in organizing your daily life.

Another study (Hölzel et al. 2008) also found that patterns of energy use in the brain associated with your immediate, physical awareness—again, the rPFC—seemed to get stronger with meditation practice, as opposed to your brain's energy being diverted elsewhere. This suggests that watching your breath and checking your posture diverts energy from the narrator's constant dialogue, helping to establish a new pattern in your brain that can feel like a quieter mind.

Wayne Drevets and his colleagues at the National Institute of Mental Health (Drevets, Price, and Furey 2008) report that the pattern of activation found in depression and anxiety associates the mPFC, likely the same area as your inner narrator, with the amygdala. It may be more than metaphor to say that your inner voice talks you into stress and distress. Drevets (2001) also found that the left amygdala seems to grow in people who are about to get depressed. J. D. Creswell and colleagues (2007) reported that mindful people seem to have a weaker link between this inner narrator and their amygdalae.

These studies demonstrate a physical connection among your thoughts, your feelings, and your physical experience of stress. The studies also suggest that becoming more mindful allows you to process your experiences differently. In your brain, mindfulness seems to bring your awareness into the present moment, instead of letting your day-to-day experiences trigger a cascade of narrative rumination, worry, distress, and physical stress. The narrator may keep talking its talk, but after sustained mindfulness practice, your brain actually has a weaker connection between this narrator and the unpleasant feelings it can arouse, such as the amount of stress you feel.

This emerging science linking the workings of the brain with the practice of mindfulness meditation suggests that we can use the ability of our brains to enact positive changes. My presentation of brain function here is by no means thorough; moreover, as time goes on, the details of the exact circuits and processes involved will grow. But this overview should give you an idea of how powerful regular mindfulness practice can be in moving your life and your relationships to happier and more secure directions.

In summary, your brain was wired to connect with others and soothe itself around the same time you began using language. In early childhood, the narrator that provides commentary on your day-to-day experiences was probably established by, and continues to be influenced by, your most important relationships with your caregivers, such as your parents. When your inner narrator takes over, it's probably contextualizing or framing your experiences in your attachment style. It seems that mindfulness can rewire some of the patterns that feed your harsh, critical inner narrator, and bring your awareness instead to your body and the here and now. The events around you may not change, but you can change how you understand, perceive, analyze, and react to them by rewiring your brain through regular mindfulness practice.

Core Practice: Narrators of Attachment

Give yourself five minutes to explore the narrator. Focus on your breath, using the silent counting of exhalations to guide you. Let the voice of your narrator unfold while maintaining awareness of your breath. Rather than count your exhalations, pay attention to this inner voice.

- What is its tone? What attitude does it have toward what it's describing?

- Does the voice remind you of someone you know?

- Now imagine how you would *like* your narrator to sound and the tone you would like it to have. Give yourself a few words of support and encouragement with this new voice.

You've just witnessed the functioning of different circuits in your brain. If you could imagine a soothing or relaxing voice, then you've also witnessed the capacity to rewire or reaffirm some of the attachment patterns that were established in your early childhood that can bring you more happiness now. If you found yourself unable to do this, keep trying. It will happen eventually.

being content

$f$rom my perspective, one of the key lessons of attachment theory is that you have to learn how to soothe yourself so that you can be mentally and emotionally free to explore and make the most of your world. No person or thing can give you happiness or a good life. These are rewards that only you can find in your own life. Yet you may feel that the details of your life get in the way of being happy and content.

distress tolerance

Do you become more easily aggravated, frustrated, irritable, or angry than you would like? Do you find yourself driven to tears, feeling overwhelmed or exhausted by things that seem to feel minor to other people? If you're prone to rumination and worry, you probably do. Your stress response and your inner critic feed off each other, spending all of your emotional energy so that there's none left for happiness and joy. One of the things that emerges with both secure attachment and regular mindfulness practice is a skill that psychologists call *distress tolerance*, which refers to the degree to which you can maintain your peace of mind, equanimity, and focus in difficult situations.

Nothing can trigger your stress response quite as easily and in the same way as that inner voice that dictates your rumination and worry. As long as your stress circuitry is easily kicked into gear by whatever may or may not happen to you, disrupting other thoughts, feelings, and behaviors, the happiness you long for will be out of your reach. Happiness will be unreliable, brought to you by the whim of things outside of your control. With the only life you have, the one you're living, the choice is yours: do you want to apply your effort to feel worse or better than you already do?

Higher distress tolerance offers you the opportunity to create opportunities for happiness by getting in control of the direction your mind moves toward. People who have a relatively high distress tolerance aren't easily frazzled by trivial stresses. They don't easily blow events out of proportion, and seem to be able to enjoy life more. Everyone has limits, but people with very high distress tolerance may find it easier than others to focus their energy on happiness and well-being. Fortunately, distress tolerance, like reading and writing, is also a skill that can be learned.

taking it step by step

You can compare it to life training. There are things you do, perhaps as major as your job or hobby, or as incidental and seemingly simple as reading and writing, that you once didn't know how to do. You had to learn how to do these things, and you had to learn step by step. Yet over time, your ability to do this job or hobby, or to read and write, has improved. Years later, it seems almost second nature. Distress tolerance and, generally, all of the mindfulness skills, are just like these other skills and practices you mastered with regular practice and effort.

Distress tolerance is crucial to your long-lasting well-being. If you're easily shaken by the inevitable stresses of life, you'll have a very hard time tapping into positive feelings. Happiness will be even more fragile than it already is. Each day will unfold like the last, and the well-being you long for will only move farther back on the horizon, chased away by the latest petty crisis in your life. The distress tolerance that arises from mindfulness practice can open the door to greater well-being by giving you a steady center in the midst of life's unavoidable stress and turmoil. This steady center can feel a lot like the secure, stable base discussed in attachment theory.

transforming distress

Most people want to be happier, and you're certainly no exception. Feeling depressed or anxious is usually not a conscious choice; typically you wind up there against your wishes, and it's hard to find your way out again. If your happiness is to be freed—liberated from the things happening to you—then it has to emanate from your own inner freedom. This is the inner freedom to realize that happiness is a choice, not always handed over on a silver platter with great fanfare. Sometimes you don't even see it coming.

Rumination and worry are infertile soil for planting the seeds of happiness. Whatever happiness comes out of rumination and worry is like a stunted plant, struggling to eke out a viable existence in the parched ground of stress and anxiety. Learning and practicing distress tolerance skills is an alternative. When the troubles of life go on around you and your steady, mindful center can maintain itself, the conditions for cultivating happiness and well-being are much more hospitable.

By freeing yourself from the tyranny of only being able to react to your life's events with heightened distress, you can begin to explore other inner narrators. By repeatedly witnessing the harsh, stress-inducing inner dialogue of rumination and worry while maintaining mindful awareness of your posture and breath, your mind may begin to distance itself from this narrator it has become identified with and become more identified with the voice that tracks your breath. This is the voice that comes from your mindfulness practice, a soothing voice that's characteristic of the stable, secure attachment base.

the road to happiness

This soothing voice stands no chance of being heard if the four-lane highway in your brain between your inner critic and your stress response remains well maintained. Tearing up this highway and establishing new pathways using regular mindfulness practice doesn't make stressful things disappear from your life. Rewiring the connection between your stress response and your inner narrator *does* change how you react to stress, and then how you treat yourself and others. Paying attention to this emerging soothing voice can help break the cycle of stress that's such a big part of your life. Rather than react with the familiar, well-practiced rumination and worry, you can begin to experience much more enjoyable states of mind.

The process of rewiring the connection in your brain and responding to stress in a new way is part of the creation of this new, soothing narrator. When my patients come in one day, after having practiced mindfulness for some time, and tell me they were cut off by an aggressive driver and found themselves laughing instead of honking, swearing, and lashing out, I know that they've made big steps in rewiring their brains. Further evidence of this rewiring comes when they're faced with someone or something that has always made them nervous and they report that they actually enjoy themselves instead.

I believe that when you see these types of changes happening in your own life, you can probably assume that the stress-inducing link in your brain between your medial prefrontal cortex and your amygdalae has been weakened by your dedicated efforts. This isn't to say that the link is gone but that your brain is trying to engage your mind in helpful ways that provide you with more opportunities to experience more happiness, less stress, or both. Sustained practice and continued training will help create more opportunities and make the new connections stronger. You'll feel better.

the wake-up call

For many of the cancer patients I work with, the experience of a life-threatening illness can often feel like a wake-up call to pursue and master distress-tolerance skills. Many people who've gone through the experience of illness say pretty much the same thing: feeling how fragile life is made them realize that "sweating the small stuff" was a waste of precious time. For these people, fighting cancer empowers them to exercise the right to prioritize what they choose to invest their time and energy in. Most choose to focus on happiness for themselves and their loved ones, and come out of the experience with a renewed vigor and zest for life.

For these patients, each day is a gift, and feels like a gift. They realize that choices we make in how to go about living can lead us to happiness or to misery. One of my patients, Lucy, had a vivid experience of this realization. Lucy had had a hard life. At age fifty-seven, a lifetime of heavy drinking and smoking made her look much older. Clean and sober for ten years when I met her, she had recently been diagnosed with an aggressive, metastatic adenocarcinoma of her lung. From the beginning, she knew that her outcome probably wasn't going to be good, and she lived for only a year after her diagnosis.

Lucy lived with her husband of fifteen years, and together, they enjoyed a simple life. He'd had his own struggles with alcohol, and for both of them, decades spent in addiction had alienated their families. They had each other and little else. Because of her illness, Lucy had to quit her job as a waitress. Around this time, she started coming to therapy to help mend some of her destructive habits and to help find the happiness that she felt had eluded her all her life.

From the start, it was apparent that Lucy had had a difficult relationship with her mother. Her father, who was the parent she was securely attached to, had died when she was young. Her mother had quickly remarried and made it clear to Lucy that she was a burden on the new family her mother wanted to start with her new husband. Lucy swallowed this pain as a child—and later swallowed a liter of vodka and smoked two packs of cigarettes every day for thirty years to silence the worry, rumination, and anger that controlled her life. After decades spent in the fog of intoxication and addiction, she had no more control over her mind than on the day she'd started drinking.

In therapy, we began to work toward mindfulness skills, such as raising her distress tolerance in order to address her harsh inner narrator. Lucy felt empowered when she learned that the voice of her mind wasn't always right and was a product of her troubled life and poor choices. Her inner voice seemed to excel in re-creating troubles, making her sustained sobriety a struggle. She discovered that long after her mother's death, her mother's voice was still with her as her inner narrator, badgering her, harrassing her, and robbing her of enjoyment each day. She became empowered to try to change the scripts she followed.

Once Lucy became aware of her potential to change by regularly practicing mindfulness skills, she began to have spontaneous moments of clarity. One day, she came to me to report that the day before, she had felt the best she'd ever felt in her life. The occasion was a sunset. She was walking down the street after one of her daily outings, when she looked up to see the dramatic play of colors that often accompanies summer sunsets in south Florida. She felt a tremendous joy and inner peace in being fully present for this particular evening.

Lucy understood that it wasn't the sunset itself that had moved her, but her experience of it. Her life was still in jeopardy in that her family situation had yet to be mended, and she and her husband had no money; yet Lucy was there for a completely joyous, ordinary moment. When I asked her what she had normally done around sunset, she tearfully reported that she was usually working at that time or else consumed by her inner dialogue. She had barely noticed sunsets. She'd had little distress tolerance to withstand the distraction of her inner narrator. From that day on, each sunset became a reminder to Lucy that presence and happiness were choices she had to make in order to feel the good things life has to offer, no matter what the circumstance. Despite her limited life span, Lucy was, in her own words, present for more happy, ordinary moments in her last year of life than in the previous fifty years.

For a lot of people like Lucy, the profound decisions they make about changing their attitudes, behaviors, and beliefs because of illness makes the rest of their lives happier. Instead of perpetuating more stress and suffering, distress tolerance allows you to witness and engage in difficult experiences while maintaining an emotional center that perpetuates your well-being. It's as if the harsh narrator were a menacing drill sergeant whose bullhorn has run out of batteries. Trained to push you into quick action and reaction with disregard for consequences, he's all of a sudden powerless to try to intimidate you into the familiar maze of rumination and worry. The drill sergeant, and all of his unrelenting standards of perfection and knack for criticism, is gradually replaced by a supportive, caring coach who inspires confidence and diligent effort.

radical acceptance

We all have a very deep desire to be happy. However, when we're not experiencing happiness in the way we want, we usually try to reject or deny whatever's in our way. When you do this, typically what you're trying to get away from isn't something that will just go away. Trying to get away from all of the suffering and distress in your life would be like trying to run away from your own shadow. Even in a dark room, it waits for you until the light of day.

Trying to get away from unpleasant situations or interactions won't address the deeper processes that keep distress around in your mind and in your life. Events pass, but your mind can hold on to them for decades. Distress tolerance doesn't mean an absence of distress or denying distress. Instead, it means getting through unpleasantness, discomfort, and negative feelings while making mindful, conscious choices about your behavior and how you'll respond to distress.

The mindful path doesn't ask you to choose between surrendering to your distress and pushing it away. The mindful path asks that you accept the conditions of your life as the only vehicle you have for improving the quality and meaning of your life. You only have the life in front of you to work with.

As mentioned earlier, within mindfulness teachings we use the term "radical acceptance" to describe the process of practicing distress-tolerance skills. Distress tolerance means turning down the volume and weakening the emotional power of your inner chatter, which is the voice of worry and rumination. Rather than push stress away or wallow in misery, radical acceptance asks that you use each day of your life as part of a solid foundation for your immediate and future well-being.

If you try to get away from stress, you make it the center of your existence. Stress becomes the reference point of your life's compass, because your life is about moving away from it.

The perspective of radical acceptance is different. If you use radical acceptance, you're placing well-being and happiness at the center of our existence. Your life is about moving toward contentment.

We usually think of acceptance as something passive, but radical acceptance is a call to action. Radical acceptance doesn't ask that you surrender to distressing situations or interactions but, instead, that you accept your burdens as your starting point for creating positive change. If you're a battered spouse or partner, radical acceptance doesn't mean that you should accept your partner's abuse. It means that you should accept the reality of your situation so that you can change things now rather than just hope that change will fall into your lap. Similarly, if you're a drug addict, radical acceptance doesn't mean that you should accept your cravings and give in to them. Instead, radical acceptance asks you to accept the reality of your addiction and, instead of waiting to hit a new high or low, begin *now* to make the changes in your life.

What's So Radical About It?

Radical acceptance is one of the richest gifts of mindfulness practice, involving deliberate use of your mind's ability to change itself. Your goal with this change is to have a greater capacity and control of the joy and well-being that's your birthright. Radical acceptance is the alternative to constant high stress, worry, and rumination. Rather than fear or anxiety, it's the absolute openness with which you experience life.

To practice radical acceptance, many Buddhist and other spiritual teachers advise that you first become intimately connected with the realization that life is impermanent and unpredictable. You don't have to have cancer in order to seize being present for precious moments or to find happiness in the most ordinary of places.

If only... We go through days convinced that we have time to worry, time to fantasize about better days, time to figure things out, and time for life to take a positive turn. If only you had more money. If only your parents had gotten their act together. If only that person hadn't been so critical or rude. If only traffic had been better. If only the weather had been nicer. If only you had been given more time. If only this or that had or hadn't happened, it would have been a perfect day.

Start now! Radical acceptance comes from a belief that you can't wait for tomorrow or next week or for the endless list of "if-only's" to be fulfilled to begin to improve your life. You have to start right where you are, with all that you are, and not "if only..." You have to accept this very moment with all of its flaws and imperfections as your starting point to make the radical changes that will lead to a more enjoyable and satisfying life. The sun can't teach you to admire the sunset; you have to bring your mind into the experience of each sunset.

You have to start immediately, because you must accept the fact that life doesn't always go the way you want it to. Suffering, misery, illness, and death find us all. We're all here on borrowed time, and none of us is guaranteed to see another day. Yet we spend our precious time running in mazes, lost in our thoughts, and worried about futures that often don't come to pass.

There's no time to waste. Suffering, misfortune, and distress find you without your having to look too hard for them. Having greater happiness in your life is what you have to look harder for. Because of the uncertainty about our longevity and the guarantee that life isn't permanent, we all have to take the opportunity to maximize the positive potential of our lives. Buddhist teachings encourage us to look for happiness and practice mindfulness with the same intensity we would use to fight a fire in our homes. Your life is at stake, and the urgency is just as real.

laying the foundations of mindfulness

From its earliest introduction to the world in *The Greater Discourse on the Foundations of Mindfulness*, the *Mahāsatipatthāna Sutta* (Walshe 1987), the practice of mindfulness has been closely linked with coming to terms with our mortality. This text is over two thousand years old and was one of the first written down after the death of the man whom we today call the Buddha. In this text, the Buddha teaches the basics of mindfulness practice that we've already covered. He teaches practitioners how to practice mindfulness using the proper posture and breath control. He also teaches how to practice mindfulness during a variety of everyday tasks, such as walking, sitting, eating, and lying down.

Next, the Buddha encourages practitioners to go to the charnel grounds that were commonplace in ancient Indian society. The "Nine Charnel Ground Contemplations," as they're called, were the first context for practicing mindfulness outside of the monastic or retreat setting. Still found in South Asia today, charnel grounds are the parts of town where people bring their loved ones who've just died to be cremated in open-air funeral pyres.

In the traditional Vedic society in which the Buddha lived, deliberately setting foot inside a cremation ground to practice meditation was a revolutionary act. Anything having to do with these places was, and often still is, considered unclean and unpleasant. They were filled with charred bone chips, stray dogs, and jackals. At all hours of the day, every day of the year, processions of weeping, inconsolable family members would bring the corpses of their loved ones amid fetid clouds of smoke and ash to be turned into dust in front of them in the always waiting arms of the cremation fire. On busy days, corpses could remain stacked for hours in the putrifying heat. Despite performing sacred funeral rites, the people who worked there were considered untouchables and shunned by mainstream society. Family members would have to be ritualistically purified in a temple—cleansed from the trip to the charnel ground—before they could return home. And yet the Buddha's disciples were encouraged to stay in these charnel grounds to begin their mindfulness practice. Each day, these early practitioners would become increasingly aware that the fire was waiting for them too, and that the day of the final trip to the pyre was coming closer and closer.

impermanence is your teacher

I understand the Buddha's sending his disciples to the charnel grounds as an act that served three purposes: First, it communicated to people interested in his teachings that they had to be serious about making spiritual progress. This was not a path for the squeamish. Second, it reminded these early practitioners that death is unconditionally accepting. Death visits everyone regardless of health history, age, gender, ethnicity, or income. Death does not discriminate, nor will it wait for what you consider the right time—it has no if-only's. Its visits are unconditional and final.

For these early Buddhists, seeing sobbing family members in acute grief day after day and seeing babies, children, young people, and the elderly all brought to and burned in the same flames taught them about death's profound acceptance of us humans and of all life. For those practitioners, radical acceptance was taught by this most merciless of teachers. They would sit there, mindful of the breath, with their minds chattering on and on just as yours does. The only prescription for coping with the sights, sounds, and smells of the charnel ground was to repeat to themselves using a soothing narrator, "None of us is exempt from this fate" (Walshe 1987, 338). Repeating this mantra in close communion with the impermanence of life allowed them to rehearse for unconditional acceptance.

Recall the first noble truth: suffering is universal. Yet suffering is also a teacher of radical acceptance. Staring into the face of death by practicing mindfulness in a charnel ground granted these practitioners the same unconditional acceptance that death seems to practice. In the flames of the funeral pyre or under the ground in a graveyard, we are all equal. There's no rank, race, gender, or income once our lives are done. We're all imperfect, bumbling humans united by heads full of chatter about hopes, dreams, and regrets. By changing their perceptions of what it means to be human using this egalitarian perspective, I imagine that practitioners of the "Nine Charnel Ground Contemplations" began to take their own inner chatter and stress less seriously. They become a little less self-absorbed.

The third and final reason why I think the Buddha urged his practitioners to practice in charnel grounds was to get a literal lesson in how short life can be. Learning radical acceptance from death instilled a deep sense of urgency in these early practitioners to commit themselves wholeheartedly to the spiritual path in order to find deep joy, contentment, and meaning in life. Once you've seen death come to all walks of life, you become aware of how fragile and impermanent life can be. Many of my cancer patients seem to undergo this same transformation. They watch as others with whom they share their battle trench get up to fight and never come back. They know that no one is exempt from the fate that mortal life has guaranteed for us all. There's no time to delay in engaging in spiritual practice to make the most of the precious days you have left.

Like charnel ground practitioners, many people who have a close and intimate brush with mortality get shaken to the core of their being. The Buddha recognized the immense power that confronting our mortality can have in motivating us to live more enjoyable and meaningful lives. Meditating on loss from the perspective of experiencing loss was so profound that the Buddha felt that it was the ultimate teacher for propelling students onto the spiritual path. After weeks of practice among the funeral flames, practitioners would leave their petty fears, transient anxieties, and deafening internal criticism and chatter behind. Not only would all spiritual teachings become absorbed in the "Nine Charnel Ground Contemplations," but so would obstacles to spiritual progress.

a deeper happiness

When you're coming from the charnel ground, life feels as fleeting as each breath. For these charnel ground meditators, I believe that the happiness they sought differed from what you and I might think of. Instead of the kind of happiness that relies on the experience of pleasure, these practitioners sought equanimity, or contentment with life. For the balanced minds of these mindfulness practitioners, creating the right conditions for happiness was as satisfying as happiness itself.

Contentment and equanimity are much deeper than the transient euphoria and pleasure we normally equate with happiness. You can think of pleasurable happiness as a treat or reward. It comes and goes, and mindfulness can certainly help you to relish these pleasurable moments of happiness by being fully present for them. There's absolutely nothing wrong with experiencing pleasure, as long as it's healthy. Often, life's passing pleasures give us sustenance to continue the journey toward deeper happiness, like a sip of water on the way to an oasis in a hot, dry desert.

Contentment is more like the secure, stable base described by attachment theory. It's nurtured by the narrator born of mindfulness, who can disarm your stress response by engaging you in radical acceptance. Like distress tolerance, contentment doesn't mean that you settle passively into complacency. Instead, contentment is treating each passing thought and feeling with equality and openness, realizing that they're as finite and transient as this precious human life.

When anger arises, the reassuring voice of your inner meditator accepts and transforms it. You accept your anger, but you are not your anger. When happiness arises, you accept, enjoy, and welcome its return. Yet you are not your happiness. When anxiety arises, you accept it without being anxious that it's there. You transform it into a reminder to take a deep belly breath and release it with your breath. But you are not your anxiety.

Just as the flames of the charnel grounds accept all life equally, so, too, can your mind accept each feeling equally. Happiness depends on things going well, but contentment is independent and free from what happens to you or around you. This attitude of equanimity is built upon the realization of impermanence.

You can remain present for moments that bring you temporary happiness, and even feel them with new intensity, and be soothed by the awareness of the temporary nature of sadness, anger, and fear. Contentment and equanimity allow you to maintain your center no matter what surroundings or challenges you're facing. This is a subtler yet more profound level of life satisfaction than trying endlessly to chase pleasurable experiences one after another. With a mind focused on contentment, you instead become more aware of the opportunities for happiness and joy all around you at any given moment. All things pass. Being mindful of this transience—and therefore preciousness—of our existence allows the mindfulness practitioner to be centered rather than carried away by fleeting emotional states.

Contentment is almost synonymous with the spiritual liberation that results from the direct experience of the nature of reality. Many people believe that the day-to-day life and reality we experience is a small part of a vast interdependent and constantly changing interplay between millions of causes and effects. We all exist in relation to each other, and when you try to absorb the vastness of all of our lives and relationships, your individual perspective captures only the tiniest part of an infinite, cosmic landscape.

True happiness lies in being mindful of the vastness of existence and recognizing the fleeting nature of our individual experiences.

Core Practice:
Distress Tolerance

When you engage in mindfulness practice, you, like countless others, may observe that you begin to notice new sensations as your session unfolds. I'm almost always confronted by a recurring itch on my eyebrow or ear when I begin my meditation session. This sort of itch seems to be part of many people's experience in meditation. In fact, now that I've mentioned it, you'll probably notice the itch or some other uncomfortable sensation as well.

When you notice the itch, you're presented with a choice and a great lesson in radical acceptance. This is the metaphorical dilemma that we all struggle with, in some capacity, throughout our lives.

- Do you change your meditative posture to scratch the itch?

- Do you sit with the itch, dwelling on it?

- Do you return to focusing on your breath?

Years ago, when I began my own practice and the itch first arose, I almost always scratched it. Then I began to notice that I would develop another one, sometimes in the same place. Other times, it would be in a different spot.

When I began to practice with a meditation group, I became more aware of my efforts to scratch the itch. It made me more self-conscious. In stretching out the time it took me to scratch the itch, I began to notice the narrator becoming anchored to the irritation my skin felt. It became the bulk of my inner commentary, but I was in a roomful of people who were sitting still. I decided not to stratch it at that instant. So I didn't scratch it. Instead, I observed my narrator becoming consumed by the itch, as I maintained my awareness on the rising and falling of my breath.

A curious thing happened. The itch went away. I didn't have to scratch it. However, another itch arose and sometimes then another. Once I chose to let them arise and diminish, I began to understand the implications of radical acceptance in my own life. The itch will always come, and it will always go. In the mindfulness session, I make the commitment to accept each itch and release it into the precious moment.

In your practice, what recurring distraction can you accept, observing its arrival and departure while maintaining awareness of your breath? Training your mind to sit with its itches teaches you to become aware of a contentment that doesn't depend on chasing pleasure.

Remember, all things pass.

wellness routines

trying to change your mental patterns isn't as simple as changing a lightbulb or changing your clothes. It's a complex process. Changing your mind to help you live a more enjoyable, less stressed life requires commitment and determination. For change to work, you must carefully create the possibilities for a healthy mind to become as self-sustaining, stable, and familiar as your ruminative and worry-prone mind feels today. Your daily life and the choices you make must help to sustain your overall well-being. Once your well-being has its own momentum, you'll feel more free to make choices about how you want to experience life's precious moments.

training for wellness

You're reading this book to help you find the path to the changes you seek. One thing I've stated in different ways is that change—teaching your mind to feel happier and your body to feel less stressed—is all about processes. The mindful path teaches us all that these changes take dedication and sustained practice. There's no finish line for any of this, and promises of quick fixes and magical cures are unsustainable and hollow.

Your body and your mind have been trained to experience life in a certain way. They'll always find these deep, stable patterns easy to come back to. Unfortunately, the fast pace of our society doesn't readily reward or encourage setting aside time during your day to meet the needs of your well-being. Faced with starting or maintaining a new routine, or going back to the worry and rumination autopilot, most of us find ourselves back on autopilot.

right effort

When it comes to the sustained practice of well-being, the ancient Taoist saying, "the journey of a thousand miles begins with one step," certainly describes things accurately. Change comes with well-intentioned, well-informed effort. Without the right amount of effort, you'll be faced with the same mind and body that you find so challenging. The time to begin to change is now.

Your progress toward a happier, more mindful existence is one that needs to be nurtured and taken care of every day, as you would a new pet or a small child. Your mind and body require the same unconditional love, limit-setting, and healthy routines, because if left to their own devices, the choices they make might not be the best ones.

Like teaching a baby or a new pet, you have to try to nurture your mind and body to make the best available choices. The mindful path asks you to be a caring parent of yourself.

The process of rewiring your brain through mindfulness practice is the necessary first step. As you learned by understanding the basics of attachment theory, your experiences as a child have a lot to do with the mind you inherited from your caregivers. Although you can't change your childhood, you can change several parts of the life you live now to help create fertile conditions for contentment, joy, and well-being.

Scientific studies make it quite clear that regular mindfulness practice can rewrite the impact of some of your childhood experiences, and also disconnect your overcritical narrator from your stress response (Creswell et al. 2007). The result for you could be a more contented life. The therapeutic dose of mindfulness practice that has been studied the most is a twice-daily practice, with a minimum of fifteen minutes of meditation at each session (Teasdale et al. 2000).

Cause and Effect

The mindful path teaches you that your happiness, health, and well-being aren't just goals that will happen someday in the distant future. They emanate from the behaviors and choices you make in your life's precious moments *today*. Mindfulness practice gives you the opportunity to answer the call to well-being by helping you to become aware of the choices you make and the consequences of those choices on your mental, physical, and spiritual health.

Mindfulness can be the cornerstone for leading a healthier life, but the rest of this healthy life is up to you. Even with the therapeutic dose, remember that mindfulness, change, and new perspectives don't have finish lines. They need constant practice, refinement, and effort. Life, in all of its impermanence, flaws, and uncertainty, is the opportunity we're all given for applying our best effort.

But awareness is not enough. This is also the time for action.

Facilitating Mindfulness

Over the years, I've come to appreciate the guidelines for maintaining the proper posture as crucial to mindfulness practice. In my experience, the basic purpose of your posture is to allow belly breaths to rise and fall gently and rhythmically as you count them off silently in your mind.

By occupying your mind and caring for your body through posture and breath, the out-of-control narrator—the voice of your stress, worry, and rumination—fades into the background. Your stress response dissolves into the balanced expanse of your breath. You create a space in your awareness for awareness itself. Mindfulness then begins to happen.

Just as your physical posture is the base for mindfulness, your daily lifestyle and routines are the base for your well-being and overall health. The choices you make in your life can provide a stable base either for your well-being or for your rumination, worry, depression, and anxiety.

the four pillars of well-being

As a clinical psychologist working in a cancer center, I have a unique perspective on how mental, physical, and spiritual health are intertwined. In working with cancer patients for many years and watching the scientific data about cancer prevention and recovery evolve over that time, a clear picture seems to be emerging of how to achieve sustainable changes in mental, physical, and spiritual health.

This means that in addition to regular mindfulness practice, a healthy diet, regular physical exercise (if your doctor agrees that you're healthy enough for it), and a good night's sleep are the building blocks of a life of well-being. A life of rumination and worry can all too easily get in the way of these essential building blocks.

I refer to these building blocks—regular mindfulness practice, healthy diet, exercise, and good sleep—as the *four pillars of well-being*. When they're in place, like the stakes of a tent planted firmly in the ground, your well-being can arise much more easily and naturally from the everyday experiences of your life. If you can, please use all of these building blocks. If you can't follow all four of them, do as many as you can to the best of your abilities. Please don't let your inability to practice with one of these pillars eclipse the benefits of the other three.

exercising mindfully

For most of us, our ancestors did a lot more physical exercise than we do. In centuries past, life was harder and shorter, but also much more active. Your ancestors didn't have to join a gym, use a treadmill, or don exercise clothes. For them, getting from the house to the job, working on the farm, and running errands was more than enough physical activity. They went to sleep physically exhausted, and woke up to do it all over again, sometimes prodded by the lash of a whip or the possibility of hunger and destitution.

Even today, for much of the world the notion of planned exercise is absurd. Without the rigors of working in fields, carrying heavy loads, and walking for miles, life's basic necessities are out of reach.

In contrast, highly industrialized countries have made tremendous strides in making life's necessities more accessible and convenient. Unfortunately, for many of us the price of this convenience is that physical activity is a choice, and far too many choose to avoid exercise or don't get enough. We have to be trained to move our bodies and pump vitality from our hearts.

Exercise and Rumination

If you're prone to rumination and worry, if distress seems too close too often, there's a good chance that you aren't getting enough exercise and would reap tremendous benefits from exercising more. Research indicates that a lack of physical activity can be tied to distressing mental activity and can literally lock in the connections among brain cells that prevent you from changing and adapting as you wish (Christie et al. 2008). Being sedentary is unhealthy for both your body and your mind, and regular exercise, on its own, can help your brain to change.

From my clinical and personal experience, I've found regular, sustained exercise and mindfulness practice to be an incredibly powerful combination in helping to alleviate depression and anxiety. Together, they help to nurture the presence of well-being, no matter what circumstances you're facing.

The challenge is always in starting and maintaining a regular habit. Here is where mindfulness can help you to make wellness routines a regular part of your life. Learning how good exercise is for you will help you. But, as with mindfulness practice, knowledge and awareness of healthy effects isn't enough; taking action is how you can make changes happen.

If your doctor thinks your body can handle it, a regular exercise routine will help your body to sustain wellness of mind. There are many types of exercise you can do, depending on your environment, resources, and health. If your health doesn't allow you to exercise, other options may be available, such as physical therapy, that you should discuss with your doctor.

You can go on fast walks, jog, swim, play sports, or go to a gym and use indoor equipment, such as a treadmill or weights. These activities are usually considered moderate or strenuous exercise. Throughout the day, you can do other things, such as take the stairs instead of an elevator or escalator, or park a little farther than necessary in order to squeeze in a little extra activity. These choices are considered mild or light exercise.

The Therapeutic Dose of Exercise

Scientific studies suggest that the therapeutic dose of exercise is thirty minutes of strenuous exercise three to five times a week. One study found that at this dose, people reported almost half as much depression after three months (Dunn et al. 2005). What's encouraging is that it's never too late to benefit from exercise. Even senior citizens who've never exercised before can benefit from the mood-altering effects of this dose of regular exercise (Antunes et al. 2005). Another study using this same dose found exercise to be as effective as therapeutic doses of a popular antidepressant drug after four months (Brenes 2007).

Think about that: exercise is literally as powerful as an antidepressant pill, but it's free and has the positive side effects of increased energy, health, and well-being!

Mind-Body Chemicals

Just as the effects of mindfulness can be tracked in the human brain, the same can be done for exercise. It appears that one of the ways by which exercise can improve your mood is by helping to regulate how your brain influences the release of substances called *cytokines*. Many researchers consider cytokines to be part of the bridge in the mind-body link (Vitetta et al. 2005). Cytokines are special cells that allow your brain to communicate with your immune system, which is the part of your body that fights off infections, helps you heal, and helps keep you healthy. There are many different types of cytokines, such as interferon and interleukin. They each do different things, such as raise your body temperature or make you feel sluggish.

When you have a cold, it's not the cold virus that makes you feel tired and sleepy. Your body's release of cytokines is what you're experiencing. The stress response stimulates the release of cytokines in anticipation of physical injury (the old fight-or-flight response hardwired into our bodies since prehistory), but this continuous release can also make you lethargic, achy, and unable to experience as much pleasure in life.

Exercise can change how your body releases cytokines so that your brain isn't always in this rut (Cotman, Berchtold, and Christie 2007). Just as mindfulness practice can help change your brain through your tracking of your belly breaths and mental activity, exercise can help change your brain through the healing that comes from physical activity.

Many of my ruminative patients wouldn't think of exercise as a way to manage stress, because they believe they would spend the exercise session lost in their thoughts, often feeling more stressed after exercising than before. However, exercise can offer many opportunities to practice basic mindfulness skills.

For instance, you can count your exhalations as you walk or jog. For a period, I counted my exhalations as I jogged, timing my runs to a certain number of breaths. Rather than getting lost in your thoughts, listening to music, or watching a television set at the gym, you can allow exercise to be a vehicle for helping you become aware of the precious moments in which you're working for your wellness and nourishing your physical well-being.

The link between exercise and mood may have seemed fairly obvious, but now we have clear scientific proof that exercise is as healthy for your mind as for your body. Exercise literally works out your mind-body system, making it easier for your brain to be resilient and protect itself from depressed and anxious states, and the worry and distress they usually bring (Duman 2005).

eating mindfully

Over the years, I've observed that when people begin exercising, they become more in touch with their bodies in general. Once this happens, you begin to make healthier choices regarding what and how you eat.

In general, a diet consisting of sensible portions that are low in saturated fats and rich in fruits, vegetables, and whole grains is ideal for optimal cardiac and general physical health. We can now also say that this kind of diet, combined with regular exercise, is good for your mood as well (Hendrickx, McEwen, and van der Ouderaa

2005). In a very literal sense, what's good for your body is good for your mind.

The food that you consume has an incredibly important role to play in your health and well-being. There are hundreds, if not thousands, of diets with all sorts of names and claims. Traditional texts usually recommend a vegetarian diet for monks and mindfulness practitioners, but in reality Buddhists follow a range of dietary practices. If vegetarianism is something that works for you, feel free to refrain from eating meat. The point is not to sell one diet to you over another. Instead, the mindful path asks you to approach each meal as an opportunity to choose wisely and to be aware of the consequences of your choices. It's about becoming aware of *how* you eat, just as the sitting practice is about becoming aware of how you think and feel.

Eating is something you're born to do instinctually. Babies are born with a suckling reflex to drink milk as soon as they emerge from the womb. Even when they can't ask, they'll put their hands, feet, and whatever might be in reach into their mouths when they're hungry. For adults in our society, food is a need that we tend to meet with convenience as a priority, and with a load of emotional baggage rather than presence and clarity.

If you're prone to rumination and worry and the cycles of depression and anxiety that they often bring, chances are that your relationship to food is one that could use some improvement. Part of depression and anxiety is that your appetite is distorted (Andréasson et al. 2007). You may frequently eat too little or too much and have a hard time feeling satisfied when you eat. To make up for this lack of pleasure, you may choose to automatically eat excessive quantities or excessively salty or sweet foods (Cohen and Farley 2008).

With regular routines such as mindfulness practice and physical exercise, I believe that your awareness will grow regarding what your body needs to eat to stay healthy. We already know from brain studies that mindfulness can help to improve your perception of your body (Hölzel et al. 2008). Exercise can help your body to feel healthy and your brain to become primed for the changes that mindfulness can bring. You can now use each meal and snack to reinforce these healthy feelings and to remind yourself of your task: to nurture and nourish your mind, body, and spirit.

When you begin to practice mindfulness, you can use your awareness to eat foods in a manner that helps your body to feel healthy. Observe mindfully how your body feels with smart food choices versus unhealthy choices.

With your knowledge about the interconnectedness of your stress level and your breathing, you can see how the dietary choices you make can influence your mood. The quality and quantity of food you eat can make it easier or harder for your body to take a diaphragmatic breath, another way in which your food choices may contribute to your stress level.

It's now time to choose to use the food you eat to nourish your well-being.

sleeping mindfully

As a ruminator and worrier, you're probably well acquainted with poor sleep. Poor sleep quality and rumination seem to have a chicken-and-egg relationship with each other: it's hard to tell sometimes which causes which. Do you stay up at night and think, or do you think at night because you're up anyway? One study, by A. J. Guastella and M. L. Moulds (2007), suggests that people who have a tendency to ruminate and worry don't sleep well after stressful events because they stay awake thinking about things longer than other people do.

Regular exercise can certainly help you get a better night's sleep. Your body has more reason to sleep since it needs the rest. Interestingly, regular mindfulness meditation can also help you to sleep better (Carlson and Garland 2005).

The importance of a good night's sleep cannot be underestimated. Sleep is restorative. Not only is it meant to help our brains and bodies repair and heal, integrate the day, and process information, but good sleep is also good for your memory (Ellenbogen at al. 2007). Regular good-quality sleep also improves your mood, and can help you to feel hopeful and engaged with others (Haack and Mullington 2005).

A Personal Example

When my first son was born several years ago, I became well acquainted with the relationship between sleep and mood. He was a difficult sleeper and, for the first six months of his life, rarely slept for more than two hours without waking up crying. Consequently, my wife and I both had chronic sleep deprivation.

After a few weeks, I could feel my own emotional resilience suffer, even with my regular meditation practice. I became much more irritable and was much more easily emotionally overwhelmed by things that normally didn't bother me. And worst of all, even if my son did have a good night's sleep, my body had become trained to sleep restlessly.

Once he became a better sleeper, I then had to train myself to be a better sleeper as well. I was able to maintain my regular meditation practice throughout this period, but now I also needed to use the same guidelines I give to my patients who suffer from poor sleep.

First and foremost, I began to exercise regularly again. Second, I followed some rules that psychologists call *sleep hygiene.* Just as the successful practice of mindfulness relies on proper posture to allow mindfulness to happen, sleep hygiene allows for good sleep to happen. I've shared these guidelines with many of my patients, and they work incredibly well for those who choose to follow them.

Sleep Hygiene

The essential points of sleep hygiene are as follows:

- Observe the same bedtime *and* wake-up time seven days a week.

- Abstain from caffeine after 4:00 p.m.

- Use your sleeping area for sleeping only. Refrain from watching TV, using your computer, talking on the phone, or reading for long periods on your bed.

- Abstain from watching violent TV shows, Internet surfing, or playing video games during the two hours before bedtime. This may mean skipping the evening news.

- Avoid heavy meals right before bedtime.

- If you're still awake thirty minutes after going to bed, get out of bed. Walk around. Go to a different room for a few minutes and take some belly breaths. Come back and try again.

- Don't keep looking at the clock.

- Wind yourself down at night with a regular bedtime routine. Take a shower or bath, put on your pajamas, brush your teeth, and use the bathroom right before getting into bed. This sends your body the cue that it's time to go to sleep. Observe the same winding-down routine every night if you can. Change out of your pajamas as soon as you can in the morning; they're only for sleeping in.

As a practitioner of mindfulness, you also have the unique ability to fall asleep mindfully. I've used the technique at the end of this chapter to help dozens of people fall asleep naturally with even the most persistent cases of insomnia.

Mindfulness and sleeping serve different purposes, even though they do overlap slightly in that they both provide healing effects. As a word of caution, sleeping mindfully is tremendously refreshing but shouldn't be considered one of your twice-daily practices. Buddhist schools believe that for meditation to change you, you have to have periods of ordinary, waking life after your mindfulness practice for there to be something to integrate. Meditation can be relaxing, but it's also meant to be an exercise that sends your mind and body a message that you're valuing their health and well-being by engaging in this regular effort.

～ Core Practice: ～
The Four Pillars of Well-Being

This set of core practices is from the *Mahāsatipatthāna Sutta*, the traditional Buddhist text in which mindfulness meditation was first written down. The first pillar is your mindfulness meditation practice. The three that follow will help to transform your life even more.

Mindful Walking

Stand with your back straight, legs slightly bent, and head looking straight ahead. Make sure that your eyes are level and that your head is being held straight.

1. Begin by taking a belly breath.

2. As you exhale, relax your body, beginning with the top of your head.

3. Notice the sensations of your body as you work your way down.

4. Where are you storing tension? How do your jaws, your shoulders, your chest, your stomach feel? Especially make sure to loosen up these areas while maintaining your erect posture.

5. Say once to yourself, silently, "I am standing."

6. Imagine all of the stress, tension, and tightness melting down from your body into the floor with each breath. Maintain your erect posture as you remain grounded to the earth.

7. After a few minutes, bring your right foot up slowly as you inhale. As you pause before the exhale, hold your foot in place for a moment. Notice your body shifting its balance. As you exhale, bring your right foot down as you take a step. Notice your body shifting its balance back to your right foot.

8. Bring your left foot up without completely lifting it off the ground as your right foot comes down, releasing the last of your exhale.

9. Now, as you inhale, bring your left foot up off the ground. Notice your body shifting its balance to your right foot. Pause. Bring your left foot down as you step,

observing your body shifting its weight back down to the left foot.

10. Repeat silently to yourself each time your foot comes down to the ground, "I am walking."

Do this for five minutes, or longer if you're comfortable with it. In meditation retreats, mindful walking is used to break up the monotony of long periods of sitting.

By doing this exercise, you can use mindfulness to let you tap into your bodily sensations as you move. Try to do mindful walking in this way at least once a week. You'll be able to check in with yourself about how it feels to be in your body and how your body feels day to day as it changes with regular exercise.

Mindful Eating

Set a plate or bowl of food in front of you. Use your belly breath as you gaze at the meal. Ask yourself silently, "How did this meal come before me?"

1. Think of the people working in the store or restaurant where you purchased this food that's in front of you, the people who made the dishes you're eating from, the people who made the utensils you're using, the people who made the table upon which your meal rests, the farmers and field hands who worked in their fields to make the meal possible, the truck drivers who drove the ingredients to where you found them.

2. Silently thank each person along the journey that made your meal possible.

3. If your meal has any animal products in it, thank the animal for the sacrifice it made to sustain and nourish your body. If your meal has plants, fruit, or grain in it, thank the plant for working so hard to produce the meal that's before you.

4. Now take a bite.

5. Hold it in your mouth for a moment. Examine the flavor. Is it sweet, salty, sour, bitter, spicy?

6. Examine its temperature. Is it hot, cold, warm?

7. Begin chewing.

8. Notice the texture. Is it hard, soft, crunchy, chewy?

9. How many times do you need to chew the food before you're ready to swallow?

10. Reflect on how many meals you've eaten on the run, gulping them down with little awareness. Observe how different it is to be present with your food, to be present with the act of eating, of nourishing your well-being each time you chew.

11. Repeat silently to yourself with each new bite, "I am eating."

Perform mindful eating in this way at least once a week. A particularly powerful variation is to start each meal in this way. You'll find that once you begin eating mindfully, starting your first bite of food in this way, you'll be more aware of your food choices.

Mindful Sleeping

To practice falling asleep mindfully, lie down on your bed at night and begin belly breathing.

1. Observe your body. Imagine a wave of relaxation spreading slowly from the tips of your toes up through your body.

2. Imagine your belly breaths pulling this gentle, slow wave of relaxation up from your feet and pushing it to every corner of your body. Repeat silently to yourself with each exhale, "I am sleeping," as this wave travels up your body.

3. Once this wave has spread to the top of your head, taking as many breaths as you need to get there, begin counting your exhalations, one by one. If you lose count, start over at one.

4. If you reach one hundred, start counting backward, one exhalation at a time.

If you wake up in the middle of the night, you can do this exercise again as many times as you need. In my clinical experience, I've never met anyone who counted the breath in this way and was able to stay awake.

~~~~~~

So many of our choices regarding what to eat, how much or how little to eat, how much exercise to get, and how we sleep are made on autopilot. Like getting into a car or bus and arriving at your destination with little awareness of how you got there, you may find yourself eating for convenience rather than for sustenance, sitting in the familiar space of tension rather than exercising your body with physical movement, and fighting sleeplessness rather than engaging in practices that will help you wake up refreshed in the morning.

Through mindfulness you can make conscious choices to get the nourishment, exercise, and sleep you need.

chapter 8

attaining meaningful goals

Setting up the four pillars of well-being creates space in your life for more contentment and satisfaction. Freeing your mind and body from the grip of rumination, worry, and distress can do even more to facilitate the presence of increased well-being. This freedom can also change how you feel about the meaning of your life.

Think for a moment about what's happening. You're becoming more sensitive and tuned in to how your body feels when going through ordinary tasks. You're more present for your ordinary daily experiences. Being mindfully aware of breathing, sitting, standing, moving, eating, and falling asleep makes these normal activities seem special, almost sacred, and worthy of reverence. As you become present for more of these ordinary moments and aware of the power of being present to appreciate everyday wonders, you find yourself having more meaningful moments.

You begin to make smart choices regarding what you do to your body and with your body, because you're more aware of how your body feels. Your mind becomes engaged in caring for your body, and in turn your body becomes like the lap of a caring parent on which your mind can sit. When your choices aren't as smart as you wish, you can forgive yourself and resolve to do better next time, instead of only feeling uncomfortable or guilty. Difficult experiences don't seem to stick to you as much as before, since you're now oriented toward the next opportunity, not just past mistakes.

teachings from the source

There seems to be something that connects your bodily awareness with your ability to be mindful so that you can begin to behave, think, and feel differently. In the *Mahāsatipatthāna Sutta* (Walshe 1987), after the Buddha instructs us in the basics of mindfulness meditation practiced while breathing, walking, standing, sitting, sleeping, and moving around, he asks us to become aware of the impermanence of our physical existence through the "Nine Charnel Ground Contemplations." But before these teachings comes a detailed body scan reflecting on all of the different parts of your body. The list is so detailed and specific as to include bone marrow, pleura, fat, mucus, and mesentery, parts of the body that aren't in our normal awareness.

That this detailed list of human anatomy is given immediately after the teachings on mindfulness is striking in light of the brain studies you read about in chapter 5. Recall that brain scans have found that the parts of the brain that sense the body become activated by regular mindfulness practice, as the harsh inner narrator diminishes (Hölzel et al. 2008). I'm not sure if the Buddha knew this was happening, but it's interesting that right after teaching mindfulness, he then gave these exact circuits in the brain an extrarigorous workout to help practitioners benefit even more!

mindful choices

I believe there's a great benefit to be reaped from meditating on each part of the body in beautiful and repulsive detail. We can understand in a concrete way that the body is an interconnected collection of tissues, bones, blood, and membranes that transforms air, water, and food into energy and produces waste products. Sensing these parts and processes can help us to develop an integrated awareness of the preciousness of our human bodies, how hard they work, and how we need to take care of them in the same way that we try to take care of our minds. This sort of awareness encourages us to view the body as a physical reality rather than an extension of our emotional desires.

When you're aware of your organs, I think you're more likely to make healthy, rather than emotional, choices for them. For instance, if you have heartburn, GERD (gastroesophageal reflux disease), or an irritable bowel, how many times do you eat something knowing that you'll regret it later? You may find that as you nurture your mind and body, you can more easily abstain from foods that irritate your system and, instead, choose foods that digest better.

The mindful path asks you to wake up to the many opportunities for health and well-being so that your actions can flow toward the health you seek. Rather than give you dissatisfaction about your body and its real or imagined flaws, the mindful path asks you to nurture and respect your body with healthy habits. By doing detailed body scans, you can also witness how transformative the four pillars of well-being can feel inside your body, in addition to your mind.

Core Practice:
Body Scan

For this exercise, you'll close your eyes and focus your awareness on each part of your body that's listed, feeling each part get relaxed and slightly heavier as your awareness passes through it. Instead of counting your exhalations, in this exercise repeat to yourself, "This part feels _____," before you go to the next part. For example, at the tips of your toes, you might observe, "This part feels relaxed"; at your jaws, you may observe, "This part feels tense"; and so on. Make your observation, relax into the feeling, and then move to the next part. I'm only using the parts of the body that you may already know. As time goes on, you may wish to add others in detail, such as the pleura and mesentery.

Prior to practicing this body scan, make sure you've used the bathroom. You may otherwise feel an urgency to go there during the practice and thereby get interrupted.

Lie down in a comfortable, quiet place. Take three deep, slow belly breaths. Extend your exhalation, pushing out the stale air from deep in your lungs.

1. Focus your awareness on the tips of your toes, sensing them relax and get heavier. How do they feel?

2. Next, send your awareness up your feet, ankles, shins, and calves, one at a time. Notice their sensations.

3. Now work your way up your knees, thighs, hips, and pelvis, one by one—bones, flesh, and skin.

4. Now notice your belly rising and falling with each breath. Can you feel your empty bladder? Can you sense your solid spine anchoring it all? Relax and continue moving along.

5. Next, focus on your lower abdomen and bowels. How do they feel? Are they empty? Are there tight spots in them? Relax and move on.

6. Send your awareness up to your liver. Can you sense the smoothness of it on the lower-right-hand side of your belly? Can you visualize your kidneys on either side of your midback? Are they relaxed as they work to keep your blood clean?

7. How about your stomach, nestled under your diaphragm and next to your liver under your ribs? Are you hungry or sated? Visualize the walls of your stomach converting your food into nutrition.

8. Bring a feeling of lightness and relaxation to your entire belly and lower back. Breathe and move on.

9. Now bring your awareness to your diaphragm, on top of your belly and then your lungs on top of it, filling up and emptying, thanks to this generous band of muscle. Next focus on your heart—large, warm, and generous. Visualize the movement of your heart and all of the rich blood pumped through every vessel in your body. Bring your awareness to your ribs and upper back, your spine. Relax your chest and your upper back.

10. Now bring your awareness to the tips of your fingers and thumbs, your hands, your wrists, all the bones of your hands and wrists. Next go to the nerves, muscles,

and tendons of your forearms, your elbows, your upper arms. How does each part feel? Relax them each, one by one.

11. Now move on to your shoulders. Relax this magical part of your body, where your arms, chest, back, and head all connect.

12. Bring your awareness to your neck, your throat, the point at which your neck meets the back of your head, the front of your head.

13. Next go to your chin, jaws, mouth. Are you thirsty? One by one, be aware of your tongue, teeth, gums, and nose. Feel the temperature of the air coming in and out of your nostrils. Sense your cheeks, ears, skin, hair, bones, eyes, and eyelids. Go to your forehead and eyebrows. Relax your brain, your skull, your scalp.

14. Take three deep belly breaths again. Extend the last exhalation, pushing out any stale air. Open your eyes and turn to your side. Lift yourself up slowly.

the nine charnel ground contemplations

After this body scan is presented in the *Mahāsatipatthāna Sutta*, what follows next are the "Nine Charnel Ground Contemplations" that every mindfulness practitioner was asked to perform in those days. You read about them in more detail in chapter 6, but let's learn some more about them here.

Recall that charnel grounds are emotionally, mentally, and physically hard places to be. They're a space that's at the peak of human suffering and distress. The sadness and anguish of grieving family members flows by in an endless stream every day and every night. The people being cremated usually have died within hours, even minutes, of their cremation. The wound of loss is still fresh, intense, and acute in their living loved ones.

Radical Acceptance of Impermanence

By becoming mindful of the universality and inevitability of death, early meditators were motivated to begin and maintain a regular practice. The instructions ask the monk to look at corpses in various stages of decay and decomposition. The only thing they're instructed to think is: "This body is of the same nature; it will become like that; it is not exempt from that fate" (Walshe 1987, 338).

In so instructing, I believe that the Buddha understood that some of the greatest potential of mindfulness meditation becomes realized in the existential confrontation between the inner narrator's ceaseless mental stream and a higher awareness of physical death. In addition to motivating people to practice regularly and attend to their own spiritual development, another reason for the "Nine Charnel Ground Contemplations" is to put the petty arguments of the inner narrator in context. Like all other beings, we, too, will one day die. Relative to death, it's obvious just how petty many of our concerns are and just how unhelpful our narrator's tone may be. Choose your stream of commentary wisely, for it's the filter through which you experience life.

The intention behind such meditations is not morbid. A constant theme in the Tibetan Buddhist traditions that I'm familiar with asks practitioners to reflect on the certainty of death and the uncertainty of when it will happen. Any day without this awareness of mortality is considered a wasted day.

This reflection is a form of radical acceptance. You're being asked to accept the deepest fear instilled in all living things: the fear of death. Being present with this fear doesn't mean to welcome or glorify death but, instead, to accept the finite nature of your existence in order to make the most of the time you have. Many spiritual traditions recognize the value of reflecting on our mortality. For instance, Ash Wednesday and Lent in Christian traditions and the Jewish High Holidays all have a focus on death, redemption, and spiritual rebirth. All of these traditions share the belief that awareness of the impermanence of the body is meant to help you come to terms with the precious fragility of our human existence, and thus to appreciate the potential of each moment.

The goal is for you to develop a secure relationship with your life. The analogy with attachment theory is that just as secure attachment makes it feel safe for children to explore the world and learn to soothe themselves in the absence of the main caregiver, the mindful path offers you the chance to enjoy exploring the world and soothe yourself as an adult in the face of your mortality.

The Result Is Meaning

These meditations on the body and its precious fragility are a further development of the central tenet of the first noble truth: suffering is ubiquitous, all around everyone, and all too easy to find. Our freedom to create happier, more meaningful lives emanates from our acceptance of this basic law of life on every level, not just the intellectual one. The harder we try to cover up the inevitability of suffering with hollow, shallow pursuits, losing hours spinning our mental wheels with imagined or insignificant worries and concerns, the more we lose opportunities to live the meaningful lives we crave. Every one of us has undergone and will undergo numerous challenges and tragedies. Acceptance of this natural law frees up the energy to transcend suffering rather than try to deny its inevitability.

Viktor Frankl's logotherapy

In modern psychology, the person who I feel has best voiced a lot of the same ideas discussed in this book is Viktor Frankl, the founder of *logotherapy*, or "treatment using meaning." In brief, Frankl was a psychoanalyst and neurologist who lived in Vienna for much of the twentieth century. At one time he was seen as the heir apparent of Sigmund Freud. However, he had a public break with Freud, because he felt that human beings were motivated as much by a need to have meaning in their lives as by the sexual impulses that Freud had expounded upon at length.

In the 1930s, Frankl was rising to prominence in his native Austria and abroad. Just before he was about to publish his breakthrough work, he was sent to labor and concentration camps along with Jews, communists, gays, and gypsies from Austria. In his book, *Man's Search for Meaning* (2006), first released in 1956, Frankl writes how one day he had a spontaneous, almost mystical type of experience, an epiphany on the nature of meaning and human life. This happened to him at the end of a day of forced labor cleaning the crematory ovens at a Nazi death camp.

an epiphany in hell

Frankl writes of walking, chained to his fellow prisoners, along a road in the Bavarian Alps at sunset. Thoughts of his wife come to his mind, and he wonders if she's looking at the same spectacular sunset he can see. He doesn't even know if she's dead or alive. He does know that she *doesn't* know what he sees, thinks, or feels, or if *he's* dead or alive. As the lights of the villages in the valley come on, he realizes that the people in the valley don't know or don't care about his suffering. In fact, he doesn't know what has happened to anyone he used to know in his beloved Vienna. He doesn't even know if he'll be alive tomorrow or if his fellow prisoners will clean up his remains the next day. The only certainty in his life at this moment is the profound uncertainty he has regarding the fate of his loved ones and of his own future.

When I read his words, I'm filled with empathy and sadness for Frankl and his fellow inmates, and shock over the extent of human cruelty. Yet Frankl describes that instead of feeling his sadness, anger, and despair solidify, he's overcome by a strong feeling of liberation. He feels free and realizes that in this world, we're all ultimately alone, regardless of our path in life. Yet this aloneness is also liberty.

For Frankl, this sense of being alone meant that we're autonomous creatures. We aren't emotionally bound by anyone or anything more than we allow ourselves to be. On the most basic level, we're alone. With this loneliness comes the freedom to create our own meaning, and awareness of our responsibility concerning the consequences of our chosen actions and meanings. As a therapist, I help people every day who are struggling with taking responsibility for change and growth in their lives. This typically means retraining their minds to look at what they choose to do.

Certainly, Frankl didn't choose to be in the concentration camps, cleaning up after the charred remains of industrialized murder. People don't choose to develop cancer. The idea that we can choose our experiences doesn't mean that we choose traumatic things that might happen to us but, rather, that with very few exceptions, we can ultimately choose what we make of the experiences we go through. Our individuality gives us the freedom to choose the meaning we create for our lives. Frankl found, despite the best efforts of his tormentors, that he was still capable of choosing how to go through the experience and maintain his own sense of dignity.

For you, this may mean finding a meaningful way to deal with a situation outside of your control, and not sacrificing your well-being to do it. However, if you're faced with a situation in which your health or safety is threatened by abuse or addiction, I urge you to get professional help immediately. Especially in these kinds of situations, the first step toward removing yourself from a destructive context is typically the hardest, but also the most rewarding in retrospect. Aside from these kinds of situations, most of us have our private, constant onslaught of daily stress that we struggle with. It's humbling to be helped by someone like Viktor Frankl, who reported to humanity the light he found amid history's darkest chapters.

the way to freedom

What Frankl teaches is that we can use our fundamental and inherent freedom to increase our suffering or to increase our happiness. We're endowed with the ability to make choices about how we experience life. Even though they affect others around us, the behaviors we engage in and how we choose to live have consequences that we alone are responsible for. The mindful path, with sustained, regular practice, is a choice that can help you take responsibility for your own health and well-being, rather than react to the people and events around you. Again, mindfulness and happiness won't be presented to you on a silver platter. They must be pursued and seized, cultivated and harvested.

The Power of Choice

Frankl spoke of his conviction that in many instances, the difference between life and death in the camps was whether or not people felt connected to their inherent capacity to make choices and sensed meaning in their suffering. You can also make choices in the face of your own personal suffering.

When inmates began to feel indifferent to their abilities to create meaning or to feel a vacuum of meaning, death would soon follow. They would sometimes just lie in their bunks, unable to get out of bed, knowing that this meant the guards would send them to die by a variety of cruel methods.

When they chose to create meaning in some way, there usually followed a tenaciousness to keep living that sometimes appeared miraculous. Starved and malnourished, dressed in rags in freezing winter after freezing winter, these ordinary human beings with a sense of purpose and meaning could never be defeated by the guards, no matter what sorts of abuse and cruelty were thrown their way.

The lifesaving choices that Frankl alludes to weren't necessarily earth shattering. I've heard from many concentration camp survivors that sometimes they would play games in their minds just to feel some sense of control and purposeful distraction. No one could know about these private mental games, and they were tremendously empowering.

Choosing which foot to step first with or from which direction to count the lines in the grain of wood in their bunks became private victories, immune to the degradation and slavery of the camps and guards. These trivial mental tasks, practiced with an acute mindfulness born from suffering, became life-giving elixirs. Though they helped the prisoners pass the time, they were also subtle forms of resistance against the indifferent and uncaring world around them.

the meaning of meaning

What Frankl credits as the key to his survival was having something to live for, moment by moment. Meaning can be broad, as vast as the sky, but it's often small, conveyed in being present for the smallest things. The key to Frankl's survival couldn't reliably be his loved ones; as far as he knew, they were already dead. He wanted to live to publish his manuscript, which had been confiscated from him the moment he set foot in the camp. This was his life's ambition, his greatest goal and unfinished business.

To stay connected to his human ability to create meaning, he also had to have smaller, more accessible goals along the way. The possibility of his manuscript being published was abstract and far off. To experience meaning in the harsh realities in front of him meant being present for islands of beauty and joy: the sunset in a mountain valley, the rare sound of a bird through the barbed wire, the delicate light of dawn despite the terrors the day would bring.

Frankl's realizations took place in charnel grounds that served a monstrous form of human evil. These weren't the spaces of religious ritual spoken of by the Buddha. Reading about Frankl doesn't romanticize the reality of the Holocaust, but I believe it elevates Frankl's humanity. It's humbling and inspiring to think of Frankl—a gifted helper, starving, dressed in rags, sleeping on a wooden plank, and hanging onto life with the thinnest of tethers—having an epiphany about the nature of human freedom.

Ironically, the manuscript that Frankl mourned and reconstructed time and again after he arrived in the camps was never published. Whatever it was supposed to be before the Holocaust was radically different afterward. Meaning, from Frankl's direct experience, is fluid. Like mindfulness, meaning is an unfolding and evolving process, with ups and downs along the way.

Meaning Is Yours to Create

Frankl observed that like freedom, the meaning that propels us forward in life and through the most difficult of circumstances is often ours and ours alone. It's accountable to no one else, and its significance is relative. Often, meaning can be found in something that's emotionally significant only to you rather than something easily explainable. Your own personal meaning is like meeting a good friend in a large crowd. Out of all of the hundreds of people around, only one has meaning, but that meaning is yours alone. To everyone else, this person is just another face. But that doesn't diminish your friendship. It's the same with meaning; that it's yours is what makes it significant.

your goals are your choices

Part of the mindful path is being aware of ordinary moments and the chatter of your thoughts. It's your choice to be present. It's your choice to pay attention. With the sustained practice of being present, you can open yourself up to more and more of these special, meaningful moments. Your mind can maintain a healthy center by becoming grounded in its ability to create meaning.

Your ability to practice daily and sustained mindfulness, eat well, exercise, and sleep well stems from your choices throughout the day. Once your practice has become well established, it will begin to inform the choices you make. Reading this book won't be enough. Your choices and actions must be consistent with the goals of your new life.

Maintaining a regular mindfulness and well-being practice also helps you to establish and sustain other routines in your daily life. Your health-generating goals can help give your mind material to reflect on other than the stressful things that are much easier to think about. With regular, sustained practice, you can also track your progress much more easily, thus getting a sense of accomplishment and empowerment about the direction in which you're moving your life.

Keep in mind, though, that your progress isn't measured by your level of success, in having relaxing or "good" mindfulness sessions. Your progress is charted by your choice to practice mindfulness. The goal is to honor the intention and action of having each mindfulness session feed your well-being, to teach your mind to be in the potential of the present moment rather than ruminate about the past and future.

The process of meeting your practice goals is as important, if not more so, than what happens within a single session. Your mind will always have its chatter, but the mindful path asks you to choose how you experience this chatter and how to let it affect your life. By being mindful of the chatter rather than being consumed by it, you're exercising the part of you that makes choices. Your meaning-making "muscles" are getting a rigorous workout. Each day you practice one or all of the four pillars of well-being, be sure to tell yourself that you've met your goal to do something good for yourself that has demonstrable results. Each of these actions is an important step. You meet your goals—being happier, healthier, and enjoying life more—one step at a time.

meaningful activity

One of the most vivid examples of the importance of goal setting occurs every day in the hospital where I work. I often meet people who've been in the hospital for a long time, sometimes for weeks or even months. At some point toward the end of their stay, they usually get physical therapy. Time and again, I've been grateful for the selfless dedication of the physical therapists who help get people out of bed and walking after lengthy periods of being bedridden.

The effect on people's moods is dramatic. After weeks or months of being ill, helpless, and bedridden, people become almost euphoric about walking twenty or thirty feet, a distance that seemed trivial to them before their hospitalization. Every time the physical therapist walks in the room, the patient's face lights up, excited to see the person who embodies their return to health and well-being. In these situations, I see not only physical reconditioning at work but also the setting, tracking, and attainment of realistic, meaningful goals. This period of recuperation is also a mental reconditioning in which people who've felt helpless in a hospital bed for far too long begin to reexperience their inner capacity to determine their destiny by choosing and reaching their goals.

meaningful goals

For these patients, as for any of us, the total lack of physical activity can trigger or amplify depressed and anxious feelings. One of the things the physical therapists do after evaluating patients is to set goals with them. At first, the goal is to walk to the nurse's station. Once this goal is reached, the goal changes. Next, the goal is to walk to the nurse's station and back again.

You don't have to be in a hospital to benefit from the guidelines for goal setting that physical rehabilitation offers. Two main characteristics that are relevant for you on the mindful path are that, first, the goals should be realistic. Someone who has had knee replacement surgery won't be salsa-dancing the next day. The goal might be to walk a certain distance with a walker. Someone who had a breast tumor removed won't be lifting dumbbells the next day. The goal for that person might be to try extending an arm. Similarly, the goal for you might be to have a certain number of mindfulness sessions in a week, a certain block of time for some form of exercise, and a specific, realistic change in your diet, such as eliminating a can of soda or an unhealthy snack each day.

Your goals shouldn't be so grand and difficult to attain that they sabotage you by setting you up to feel defeated. If they are, get realistic. The therapeutic doses of exercise and meditation may take some time for you to maintain. Only a minority of my patients can take to them immediately. Realistically, the therapeutic doses need to be introduced little by little into your daily routines. Establishing them in your life takes time and effort; it's also a process.

Second, consider that although physical therapy happens every day, its related goals are usually tracked on a weekly basis. I think this is a helpful strategy for you too. Mindfulness emerges moment by moment, but becoming more mindful takes a lifetime of practice. If you track your progress minute by minute, or even day by day, you may not feel as much of a sense of accomplishment as if you tracked your progress every week or even every month. You'll find yourself experiencing benefits one moment at a time, but the progress you chart by comparing one week or month to another will feel even more rewarding. Setting meaningful goals starts you off on the mindful path: it's the first step toward feeling a sense of accomplishment about taking an active role in soothing your ruminative, worrying mind while generating, maintaining, and increasing your total well-being. You can then have a joyous, reassuring accomplishment to look back on—and another to look forward to—as you check on your progress.

resilience

like mindfulness, meaning unfolds and manifests whenever space is cleared for it in your awareness. And like happiness, you need to actively pursue meaning, because it doesn't always invite itself over spontaneously. For Viktor Frankl, creating meaning was a process without a finish line. He referred to it as searching for meaning, not getting or finding meaning. It's a path, a process.

Because it's a search for meaning, it's open ended, and can feed off your life experiences. Meaningful goals can be very broad, such as Frankl's desire to publish his manuscript. They can also be very specific, like being present for a sunset or sip of water. You can search for meaning in specific tasks or in fleeting moments of enjoyment. If you set specific meaningful goals, it's best to keep them realistic and attainable.

the evolution of meaning

Like all things in life, meaning can also change. It adapts to new circumstances. Like each moment, meaning is unique. It's yours to create and explore, building on what came before and pulling you forward to new directions in life.

Once Frankl published his manuscript, new horizons of meaning arose. The search continued and never stopped. For Frankl, life seemed to be a series of new horizons and adventures. He even learned to skydive in his seventies.

For you, the meaning of your life can also change depending on your own capacity for experience. Maybe you attained a meaningful goal but didn't know it at the time. For instance, many people look back on their youth or younger years with longing, because it was then when life seemed open and the meaning of their lives and purpose wasn't yet determined. The meaning of those days was that life still held promise and potential.

Yet as the years go by, many people feel as if they haven't been able to fulfill dreams or ambitions they'd hoped to. Parts of their lives, such as career or family life, seem to lack the meaning or value they'd hoped for. You may feel disconnected from your ability to live with as much meaning and enjoyment as you hoped for in your youth. This disappointment fuels hours or months of rumination, worry, and distress. It spills over so that it seems hard to get happiness out of any part of life. Moments go by and are lost while you're on autopilot.

Each moment you spend reminiscing about your youth is one spent living in the past. Today is tomorrow's glorious past that may take on a meaning later that currently eludes you. It may help you to go ahead and seek the meaning in today's moments in order to feel a sense of purpose now rather than later.

rumination, worry, and meaning

Worry and rumination seem to arise from the parts of your life that apparently lack meaning, or about which you feel a lack of power to create meaning. Typically, these are the places of minor and major suffering. This suffering can be as minor as a misunderstanding at the grocery checkout line or as major as money troubles, illness, or divorce.

For all of us, when our bodies get sick, we feel the fragility of human existence. It can take effort to use this fragility to heighten our sense of wholesome and healthy pleasure.

Our careers can take disappointing turns, and we can feel the burden of having to make money or feel let down by our career paths. It takes effort to find a way to have your livelihood increase your happiness or that of others.

You can feel isolated from other people. Friendships can seem to be just out of reach. Even thinking about being around people may make you feel stressed. It takes effort to feel joy from being around others.

A happy family life is difficult to maintain, and you might feel the stress and tension of being a product of your family history. When you're around your family, having your earliest- and deepest-set buttons pushed by those who are expert at doing so, it can take special effort to feel your freedom to make choices about how to respond.

All of life's difficult situations take effort to be transformed into meaningful experiences. Think of how it was for you to learn to read. First, you started with one letter, then you went on to one word, and then a simple sentence. Years later, you're reading this book, with all of the letters, words, and sentences strung together. But you weren't born with knowledge of how to do this. You had to train in it and then practice. It took effort at first, and now you're an expert. And you're choosing to read these words at this moment to help you live a happier, more meaningful life.

creating meaning is a choice

Searching for meaning involves a series of steps as well. You may need to start with small, concrete steps before graduating to broad goals. Some of these small steps might be to practice mindfulness skills; exercise regularly, eat well, and sleep well to facilitate physical health; donate money to charity to give your livelihood more meaning; or perhaps choose a more meaningful career track. You might choose to be mindful of your well-being when around your family and choose better behaviors to engage in around them. You have to choose to be mindful of your choices.

The search for meaning on the mindful path is an attitude toward life as much as a set of tasks. It's a choice and an outlook, an orientation toward living life's unpredictable journey. I've found in my clinical practice that although the search for meaning can have ineffable qualities, it's best to try to articulate with precision exactly what you're searching for.

For example, though "searching for happiness" is a noble goal, it's not very specific. Instead, you may want to articulate it this way: "I want to be more aware of moments that bring me happiness," or even more specifically, "I'm going to enjoy the sunset today"; or make it about something in your immediate surroundings. Your goal can even be just to take a moment to appreciate the look and feel of the room or setting you're in right now—to simply be present. Searching for meaning is about choosing presence and choosing to give meaning to something you already do or would like to do more.

Frankl realized that being present, being mindful, helps us experience meaning. I believe that mindfulness practice is an embodiment of the search for meaning itself, in that you can't feel that life is meaningful if you can't feel its individaul moments. If you're on autopilot, the moments of meaning in your life will pass you by, while rumination and worry linger. Being mindfully engaged with the search for meaning can counterbalance the distressing mental script that has dominated your life.

setting the stage for resilience

Without mindfulness and the search for meaning, you can endure suffering, but you can't grow or thrive in your progress toward your goals. Your experience of suffering is limited to distress: rumination, worry, anxiety, anger, and depression—not the meaning or growth that can come from suffering. Changing how much of your life is dominated by rumination and worry means changing the meaning of your suffering, be it the minor hassles of your life or major traumas and challenges.

When your mind is faced with adversity, it can be helpful to give yourself silver linings to focus on. When I meet people who have cancer, despite their distress, they almost always relate to me that they feel closer to certain friends and family members, sometimes to their own surprise. Cancer survivors often walk away with more passion for life or different priorities that help them and their loved ones to focus on health and well-being. One of the most amazing things I've experienced on various occasions was to have cancer survivors tell me that because of the wisdom with which they now live life, they're actually grateful for the experience of cancer.

In psychology, we call this *resilience*. An empirical study led by J. D. Teasdale (2000) shows that sustained mindfulness practice can help you to be more resilient in the face of life's challenges. For instance, people who get depressed once are more likely to get depressed again. Once the door is opened, it is reopened more easily the next time, and chances are that you'll find yourself back at some point or another. However, mindfulness seems to prevent this from happening for people who've been depressed frequently. The therapeutic dose in the Teasdale study was eight weeks of daily practice, along with a weekly group practice. The effects on depression relapse were measured after one year.

Another fascinating effect of mindfulness practice is that it may actually make your body more resilient. In an intriguing study, R. J. Davidson and colleagues (2003) found that regular, sustained mindfulness practice—one hour per day for eight weeks along with participation in weekly meditation groups—increased the electrical activity in a part of the brain associated with good feelings for up to four months. The size of this increase predicted the extent to which the immune systems of the meditators in the study were able to mobilize against a flu virus that they were injected with at the beginning of the experiment.

Not only did regular, sustained mindfulness practice make the meditators less anxious, but it also seemed to awaken positive feelings in their brains long after and made their immune systems more robust in fighting off illness. The effect of sustained mindfulness practice was a better mood, less anxiety, and better health. Again, this is only after eight weeks of sustained practice. Imagine what sustained practice might do for your life!

your mindfulness is yours alone

Certainly, mindfulness didn't change the life events of the study participants, and it won't do that for you either. You have to work with what you have. Your practice of mindfulness won't make your daily hassles disappear. People won't drive better around you after you've been practicing mindfulness. They won't communicate better after you've been practicing. And certainly, your practice of mindfulness won't negate the universal reality of the first noble truth, the ubiquity of suffering.

What mindfulness practice, along with exercising, eating healthfully, and sleeping well can do is give you the energy to adapt to both the petty and major adversities you face in your life. Rather than having your life feed the habit of rumination and worry, leading to the inevitable periods of depression and anxiety that follow, you can let it become a vehicle for your search for meaning, well-being, and happiness.

Inviting Resilience

I've found that my most resilient patients have this attitude toward life: each obstacle and setback in their lives feels more like a challenge to overcome and squeeze meaning out of than a problem to be knocked down by. Like the search for meaning and the mindful path, resilience is also a process that unfolds and emerges from life's uncertainties and ups and downs.

Resilience doesn't mean acting as if nothing has happened or being unaffected by life. On the contrary, resilience means change—but meaningful, positive change, growth in the harshest of environments, like experiencing that luscious strawberry growing on the side of a rocky cliff. Resilience doesn't hide the immensity, tragedy, or horrors of suffering. But it transforms horror into meaning.

Think of Viktor Frankl. Certainly, no one can say that his time in concentration camps was good or positive. But it was meaningful. Because of Frankl's choices, good things came for all of us from the horror and darkness that spread across the world at that time. These good things didn't come from the labor and death camps or the Holocaust—they came from Frankl. For the cancer patients I work with, resilience doesn't make chemotherapy pleasant. But meaning does give the experience purpose, and with purpose, the patient can endure the treatment a little more easily.

We all live private lives that are guaranteed to end. We're all prisoners of our mortality. Yet like Frankl, we have a deeply instilled inner freedom that's vast, untouchable, and universal. If we choose to use our life experiences to awaken and empower our liberty and ability to create meaning, even the most difficult of life's situations can be transformed into something meaningful, perhaps even spiritual.

Meaning gives you the emotional and spiritual fuel to thrive, and move closer to being the type of person you want to be. Your inner potential can shine. Rather than burn you out, the fires of life's challenges can make you stronger.

Resilience Is Spiritual

Though an understanding of the importance of meaning for building happiness is relatively new to psychology and the sciences, it's the territory of the world's spiritual traditions. Religious and spiritual teachers have long taught about finding pearls of great wisdom and opportunities for growth in the unlikely places in our lives, making the magic of resilience attainable for all of us.

I see the Buddha's teachings on the four noble truths and the "Nine Charnel Ground Contemplations" as tools for resilience. Since in his teachings suffering is viewed as a natural, universal part of all of our lives, you can use suffering as the starting point for searching for a more meaningful life. Instead of suffering being the opposite of happiness, suffering becomes the foundation from which your happiness can grow. Because the Buddha taught that suffering is universal, the opportunities for happiness are all around you now rather than waiting for suffering to take a vacation.

In the spiritual and religious traditions that arose from Abraham—Judaism, Christianity, and Islam—suffering has long been thought of as belonging to the "will of God." These traditions teach that like Job, we can't often know the reason, the meaning, of God's will, but it's up to us to either increase our faith and move closer to God in the face of our individual suffering, or move away from God and into the hell of a spiritual vacuum, a life without meaning.

I'm not advocating for a particular spiritual or religious tradition, or even for your having any religious or spiritual tradition. What I do advocate for is that you strive to search for meaning in your suffering. The meaning of your suffering is up to you, but after searching for it, you'll find that you're more resilient.

When your life, with all of its joys and challenges, triumphs and tragedies, is viewed as meaningful, you can find the strength to not only endure the ups and downs but also grow from them. In so doing, you reclaim your freedom, your capacity to choose the goal that the path of your life works its way toward.

The Qualities of Resilience

Since psychology's recent discovery of the human tendency toward resilience, we can better describe what resilient people are like. In general, they tend to have better coping skills; to be focused on the present moment and future goals rather than their past experiences or worries about the future; to be hopeful; to feel empowered to make choices, seek help, forgive others, and help others; and to focus on their strengths and skills (Glicken 2006). These are excellent personal characteristics for everyone to work toward.

I believe that mindfully engaging in the search for meaning can help you to become more resilient or to at least have more of the qualities that resilient people demonstrate. I find that the most resilient people also don't often think of themselves as resilient, so chances are that you'll actually be resilient long before you think of yourself that way.

the challenge of forgiveness

In the context of the mind that's prone to rumination and worry, the hardest of the resilient qualities to train for and practice is forgiveness. Not coincidentally, the world's spiritual and wisdom traditions have also emphasized the central importance of forgiveness.

For instance, the Christian prayer known as the Our Father specifically asks God to "forgive us our trespasses as we forgive those who trespass against us." The Buddhist seven-limbed prayer has within it a confessional to forgive yourself and others on a daily basis.

In the Buddhist tradition, as in other spiritual teachings, the importance of forgiveness is not only to free up emotional and spiritual energy, it's also an exercise in the highest and most difficult aspiration for human beings: compassion. Not to be confused with pity, compassion is the exercise of radical acceptance. Compassion is to feel for and feel with another being, as if that person's welfare and well-being were your own.

Interestingly, for those of us with anxious, avoidant, or insecure attachment styles, compassion and forgiveness may be harder than it is for others because of our excessive rumination and worry (Burnette et al. 2009). The ruminating mind seems to block the capacity to forgive and care for others effectively. Instead, it's easier to be vengeful or hold a grudge (McCullough et al. 2001).

But getting angry or frustrated at others or against your own mind isn't the answer. Your mind already knows how to do that to itself and others quite well. A better alternative is to turn to your mind with compassion, or radical acceptance, and love, the kind of love and caring that you would like for others to show you. In resetting your attachment style, you can become more compassionate and helpful (Mikulincer et al. 2005). You can nourish your own mind with compassion so that it can then share compassion with others.

 ## Core Practice:
Loving-Kindness

In the Buddhist tradition is an incredible set of exercises known as *metta*, or loving-kindness. Metta is where radical acceptance and forgiveness meet, and at their intersection is unconditional love. Keep in mind that this doesn't mean that you have to like everyone. Unconditional love is opening your heart to all of life. Loving-kindness is a choice. Like happiness and mindfulness, feeling in touch with your own inner freedom won't present itself on a platter to you. The sense of your inner freedom from forgiveness and radical acceptance needs to be cultivated and comes from regular practice.

For this exercise, find a comfortable, quiet spot.

1. Close your eyes and take three deep, slow belly breaths.

2. With the first breath, become aware of your surroundings.

3. With the second breath, become aware of your body and your posture. Extend the exhalation with a sense of pushing out any stale air from the base of your lungs.

4. With the third breath, become aware of the breath itself.

5. With your eyes still closed, visualize your body. As you imagine your body, inhale, saying to yourself, "May I be free from suffering."

6. As you exhale, say to yourself, "May I be at peace."

7. Practice for a few breaths in this way.

8. Now, imagine a loved one, perhaps a child, a family member, or a dear friend. If you can think of no one else, it can be a pet or someone you don't know who you imagine to be suffering.

9. As you inhale, silently express this wish for that person: "May you be free from suffering."

10. As you exhale, silently express this wish for that person: "May you be at peace."

11. Practice for a few moments in this way.

12. Now, imagine someone who has caused you harm, someone who has caused you to hurt or suffer. As you inhale, silently express this wish for that person: "May you be free from suffering."

13. As you exhale, send the person this wish: "May you be at peace."

14. Now, imagine our magnificent, vast planet Earth. Imagine all of the teeming masses of humanity, all of the animals, plants, and insects. As you inhale, send the

planet and every living thing on it the wish: "May we all be free from suffering."

15. As you exhale, send planet Earth the wish: "May we all be at peace."

16. Practice for a few moments in this way.

I know that this exercise can have an incredibly profound effect on you, no matter what your circumstance or unique life history.

One of the most poignant and moving experiences I've ever had as a psychologist was facilitating a metta practice session for a roomful of parents whose children had been murdered. Few of us can fathom tragedy and suffering at this level.

Yet at the end of the session, many participants walked up to me with tears streaming down their cheeks. They all told me that the metta exercise allowed them to feel the capacity to meditate and grow spiritually again, even many years after the death of their children. Although I hadn't specified whom they should visualize, most of them chose to visualize the person who had murdered their child. After practicing metta, although they certainly did not excuse what the murderers had done, they felt the liberation of spiritual forgiveness, whether or not they were religious. These parents felt the freedom to connect with the memories of their murdered children without the baggage of anger and hatred toward the murderers. In practicing forgiveness toward someone they hated, they were able to feel a purer love for their children.

forgiveness is a choice

Though the freedom to forgive and love is priceless, it's accessible. You have a choice in how to spend your emotional energy: imprisoned in your past sufferings or free in the present moment. Forgiveness gives us the freedom to be resilient and thrive in the face of suffering.

In my clinical experience, I've found that people who tend to ruminate and worry actually have an easier time forgiving others than forgiving themselves. You tend to be harder on yourself than on other people. So forgiveness doesn't just mean forgiving others who you feel have caused you suffering, but also forgiving yourself for any of your past or future mistakes and poor choices.

For example, as I've stated before, it can be quite difficult to establish wellness routines in your life. Garnering the ability to do so is a process, complete with ups and downs. Do you get anxious, angry, or frustrated at yourself for being unable to establish or maintain your wellness routines? Does the thought of it make you ashamed, embarrassed, or annoyed?

Do these negative feelings help you to feel happier? Chances are they don't. Forgive yourself. The mindful path is a process to be taken one step at a time.

Forgiveness Is Freedom

Forgiveness of others doesn't mean devaluing your own suffering, forgetting how cruel others may have been to you, or enabling their future unhealthy behaviors. If you've been abused or assaulted, certainly remove yourself from the situation and seek justice. In these sorts of instances, forgiveness is *not* forgetting.

For me, forgiveness is about freeing yourself from the power others have over you, liberating your capacity to feel, and liberating your feelings from what others have done or what you've lived through.

Remember, forgiveness is freedom, your own freedom. It's releasing the emotional connection you may have to the distress of your suffering and moving yourself to create meaning, grow, and find a happier way to live.

The freedom that forgiveness and resilience can bring can also mean freedom from rumination and worry. For most people, what you ruminate and worry about is unfinished business: the what-ifs of the past and future, stressful conversations, petty hassles and major tragedies, and the parts of your life that seem to lack meaning. Practicing metta and moving yourself to a place of forgiveness helps you to silence your ruminative mind with the self-soothing action of loving-kindness. Metta can give your ruminative mind a rehearsed script to anchor it down rather than let it drift this way and that in the sea of anger, vengefulness, and distress. Metta is a sobering, grounding element to the bitter intoxication that can carry away your happiness and well-being. Metta can be your nurturing caregiver, comforting your mind and letting the heavy chains of past wrongs and hurts fall off of you.

on the road to compassion

All of the world's great spiritual and wisdom traditions present compassion as one of the central goals of human life. If you believe in heaven or hell, you believe that good deeds will lead you to a pleasant afterlife and that unkind deeds are evil, leading you to damnation. For people who believe in reincarnation, good deeds are the ticket to an auspicious rebirth, whereas bad deeds are a path to a lower existence. Even many atheists and agnostics believe that good deeds are crucial, precisely because there's no deity to watch over us; our choices may have even more value when they're done for their own merit, their immediate earthly consequences, rather than a future reward.

Whenever we speak of good deeds, the general understanding is that it means behaving morally and ethically but also compassionately. What do you think of when someone says so-and-so is a "saint"? Chances are, kindness, warmth, and compassion come to mind.

However, compassion is not only the domain of saints and legends. Great people are worthy of adoration but not at the cost of your own spiritual progress or mental health. The potential for resilience, forgiveness, and compassion exists in all of us.

In one of his teachings, His Holiness the Dalai Lama (Gyatso 2004) relayed the story of Milarepa, the revered eleventh-century saint from Tibet. After a tumultuous youth as a rebellious and murderous thug, Milarepa meets his spiritual teacher, Marpa, the great translator.

Taking Marpa's teachings to heart, Milarepa begins his meditation practice in earnest. Years later, at the end of a long life of giving spiritual teachings all over Tibet, Milarepa has the premonition that he'll soon die.

Gathering his students and disciples together, he says his good-byes and answers their questions one final time. One of them asks him, "Are you a god or a Buddha?"

Furious, Milarepa gets up and shows his students and disciples his buttocks, revealing his calluses earned from years of meditation practice in remote caves and on high mountain peaks. "You see these? This is what I am. What I am comes from practice. I'm not a god. I'm not a Buddha. I'm just a man, a man who has practiced."

Milarepa tells all of us, from the end of his days so long ago, that the transformation that changes you from your familiar suffering to a meaningful, compassionate life, perhaps even a joyful life, is within any human being's grasp. This path is a question of choice: how you choose to spend your time and what goals you choose in life. Milarepa's challenge to us is this: are you willing to try?

chapter 10

perfecting the process

by now, you've had some experience practicing mindfulness. You've observed that mindfulness doesn't mean having a quiet mind but, rather, having a present and accepting mind. You've had the opportunity to notice that mindfulness isn't the same as silencing your thoughts but is about watching your thoughts without being enslaved to them. Mindfulness is a door that lets you out of the stuffy room of rumination, worry, anger, and anxiety, and into the fresh air of the here and now, into a more compassionate and healthy life.

Mindfulness, the search for meaning, and other broad goals like health and well-being are processes. Rather than a single finish line, they have many mile markers along the way. You can search your whole life for mindfulness, meaning, health, and well-being, but each day the journey begins again. Like one tile in a mosaic or a tiny detail in a large painting, individual moments may look small, even insignificant, close up. But when you look back on a lifetime of choices and practices built moment by moment, a beautiful picture can emerge.

the mindful path is a new beginning

The goals this book has invited you to set for yourself are about growing into a different way of living and being than you've been used to for far too long. You already know how to drive yourself into distress. You have solid experience doing that, and even though it may come easily to you and be familiar, it hasn't made for the joyful kind of life that you hope for.

Process goals like searching for meaning, health, and well-being are about valuing your ability to grow unconditionally. Your potential isn't in the quality or quantity of your rumination and worry. You have the same potential for growth regardless of your age, your obstacles, your mistakes, or your distractions. Your choice of inner peace leads to your becoming a more compassionate person to yourself and to others around you. This quality is characteristic of those who value the meaning each day can bring, and respect their own precious human lives enough to make choices consistent with learning and growing into new and improved people every day.

And it all begins in a single moment and continues one breath at a time, one bite at a time, one night at a time, and one step at a time. Each moment and each breath are like a small piece of colored tile that you assemble with others to make the mosaic of your joyful, mindful, and meaningful life. Each moment is as precious and full of potential as you choose it to be.

concerns about mindfulness

Over the years, I've heard some people suggest that practicing mindfulness makes you a boring person or robs you of your personality. Because of the way your mind has worked, you may have developed some unique behaviors, expressions, and wit that are funny and attractive. Although your mind might drive you crazy, it may also be the source of your charm and humor. One of the myths of the mindfulness path is that you'll lose this uniqueness and even possibly become zapped of your drive to succeed and improve.

This doesn't have to be the case. Certainly, as your mindfulness practice matures, you become more comfortable in your own skin. This may change some of your behaviors, but probably only those that emanate from your discomfort or excessively critical judgment of yourself. More than likely, mindfulness will allow you to lose unhelpful behaviors while you gain a new appreciation for the quirks and uniqueness that give you character.

One of the goals of the mindful path is for you to make the practice your own, rather than try to act like or be anyone else. It's certainly not about losing excitement from your life or reducing your drive to succeed. The mindful path is about how to achieve your goals in a way that leaves you joyful, peaceful, and less anxious and worried than you are now. Mindfulness is about being yourself and being *okay* with being yourself.

Your mind learns to develop an accepting, nurturing relationship with you, one that perhaps you didn't see modeled by your parents or early caregivers. Your mind allows you to be you. In practicing the art of being present, you learn how to experience more of life's excitement and potential without being thrashed about by its ups and downs. Your mind, your breath, your choices are all parts of the stable base that steers you toward your goal: a happier, healthier *you.*

Rather than fight with you using endless chatter and criticism, self-loathing, guilt, or angst, your mind can learn to welcome your experiences, creating confidence in your ability to meet your goals and challenges. You may certainly continue to experience fears and doubts, but these gradually rise and fall away without leaving a deep impression on your sense of self. You can forgive others and yourself for having created or perpetuated your mind's pitfalls and traps. Your doubts and stresses may remain, but they likely will be mere shadows of their former power, distant reminders of a more frustrating way of life that you're moving beyond.

own your mindfulness

When the Buddha taught mindfulness meditation and all of his other teachings 2,500 years ago, he didn't restrict them. He didn't say you had to be a monk or belong to his cabal to benefit. He didn't declare that you had to pay a fee or get certified to practice mindfulness.

In fact, he routinely challenged anyone who heard his teachings to put them to the test. If someone else's diligent practice and following of his teachings led to enlightenment, then his teachings could be considered valid. If they didn't lead to enlightenment, then they weren't worth the palm leaves they were written on. He declared with tremendous open-mindedness that if some or all of his teachings were found to be false for someone, the teachings should be ignored and discarded.

For you, this means that you have to put mindfulness to the test in your life, rather than take my word for it or simply read about it. We hear of many practitioners who've found enlightenment by practicing the Buddha's teachings. But the stories of other practitioners will do you no good if you aren't putting their methods to practice in your life. Meditation masters can inspire and motivate you, but they can't help you unless you try to do what they've done.

Mindfulness is yours to mold, shape, and make into a grounded version of your own uniqueness. You don't have to fit into any stereotype or expectation of what a mindfulness meditation practitioner is like. You don't have to dress the part or follow the latest fad in meditation accessories. Tibetan Buddhist teachers traditionally requested that practitioners keep the details of their practice secret to avoid coming across as arrogant or conceited. Your experiences on the mindful path are yours alone, a celebration of your freedom, autonomy, and individuality.

Your experience of this precious moment is yours, not mine or anyone else's. You're free to be an individual in the mindful experience of what's happening in your awareness right now. This is the activating force behind the Buddha's teaching: making the practice *yours*.

Your practice will differ from mine, just as mine differs from that of the teachers who taught me. The material you're working with, your personality, also differs from mine. Yet I can say with some certainty that some things that bothered you before probably don't bother you now. This may surprise and even puzzle some people around you. Our families and friends have come to know us over time and have some expectations of how we behave.

But the changes in your mind that leave you happier and less distressed don't have to rob you of your personality. Instead of making your behavior and emotional life appear to be flat and dull,

I believe that mindfulness practice can enrich your overall enjoyment of life. There's no false choice between being interesting and being dull. Mindfulness is about enjoying your life's moments rather than struggling with life's high peaks and low valleys. It's about appreciating your ability to feel rather than being invested in whether those feelings are good or bad.

The emotional stability that's one of the main benefits of mindfulness doesn't mean that you don't feel emotional changes or that nothing fazes you. It means that rather than base all of your happiness on specific outcomes, you're more in touch with and accepting of your capacity to feel, think, and act.

Think of two people watching a horse race. One's a gambler who puts all his money on one horse. The horse loses, and he's financially ruined. For this gambler, the race is very distressing, because that particular horse didn't live up to his expectations. He goes home despondent, broken, worried, angry, and depressed. Losing the bet eclipses any excitement or enthusiasm he felt for the race.

The other person watching the race simply loves horses and doesn't place any bets. He wants to see different breeds racing and to compare their gait, speed, and grace. He cheers his favorite on, but no matter who crosses the finish line, this fan has a great time. He's there for the joy of the experience, not because of one horse or the other. For him, the race is exciting and thrilling. He recalls the excitement of the crowd and the skill of animals and riders; who won the race is incidental. He goes home with the joyful memory of this contest of strength, agility, and speed. He accepts the outcome because he was there for the whole experience, not just to see the winner.

moving toward a mindful life

Mindfulness is about approaching reality with an awareness that all living beings, including you, are precious, unique, wondrous, and evolving. Think of the "Nine Charnel Ground Contemplations." All human life is fleeting—yours, mine, and that of everyone you know. In the face of your mortality, the importance of finding joyful moments in your life that help you grow and live fully is even more crucial.

The stable base of unconditional love for your ruminating and worrying mind is the foundation for moving you along the mindful path to experience each of life's precious and meaningful moments.

How to Get There

There are two different ways to reach your goals: to move toward a goal you want or move away from a goal you don't want. Trying to get away from your mind and its habits of rumination and worry may have motivated you to explore the mindful path. Now that you've read about and experienced some of the things I've described, and know the verifiable effects of mindfulness, the time has come to set a goal to move toward.

The mindful path is the active process of moving toward your goal, away from anxiety and depression at first but then toward more happiness, joy, and awe. The mindful path is your movement toward wellness.

The four pillars of well-being—practicing mindfulness, exercising, following a healthy diet, and getting good sleep—are meant to recharge your batteries and teach you to make conscious, meaningful choices in securing your daily happiness and well-being. They aren't meant to deaden your experience of life but, rather, to heighten your ability to engage with life instead of allowing the fight against your mind to cause you to miss meaningful moments. These practices help you make deliberate choices in building your life as you want it to be, rather than focus on tearing down what you don't want.

why people stop practicing

"I'm still stressed!" One of the misguided assumptions of people who've recently begun meditating is the expectation that all stress will disappear. Disappointed, new meditators come in my office and tell me that they had a stressful experience: they're surprised that despite being inoculated daily with mindfulness practice, they find stress creeping back into their lives. I urge you not to make the same mistake some people do, to discard the practice after you hit your first "speed bump" along the way.

Stress is a natural part of all of our lives, just as are anger, frustration, joy, and awe. Mindfulness is a tool, not a weapon. You can't destroy stress with mindfulness, but you can manage it better. Mindfulness won't prevent stressful events from happening, but it can help you become more aware of how you react to stress and help you find better ways to respond.

"It's not relaxing enough!" Mindfulness can help you become more relaxed, but sometimes it's not a relaxing practice. Your mind wanders. Your mind will always wander. That's the nature of the mind. Sometimes you're present for disturbing thoughts, unpleasant fantasies, and uncomfortable sensations. Even after years of practice, some sessions can be almost impossible to sit through. Distraction or unpleasant things can still take hold during the empty space of mindfulness sessions. What changes is how your mind, brain, body, and behaviors react to your mind's inevitable wanderings.

The process of sitting down, walking, or engaging in other applications of mindfulness practice on a daily basis rewires your brain to experience equanimity and unconditional love toward your life's precious moments. Judgments, ruminations, and worries take a backseat to your appreciation of making healthy choices regarding your behaviors and priorities. Being compassionate and forgiving of yourself and others can be relaxing, but the process begins with sitting through your mental, physical, and emotional distractions.

Good Things Can Come from Rough Times

Mindfulness is at its most impressive when it alters those sessions where you feel that you're the worst meditator ever. Your determination in sitting through these sessions empowers your mind to set healthy goals and pursue them tenaciously, no matter what. You send yourself the message that your goals are worth pursuing because your precious life is one worth enjoying, not just one to settle for.

Your difficult sessions—when you lose count of your breath, the phone rings, that darn itch in your ear or eyebrow won't go away, the room seems too hot or cold just as you settle in, or your mind is completely unfocused and distracted—can fuel your dedication to being proactive in choosing your life's direction and meaning. When you sit through these tortuous sessions anyway, you're telling your mind that your well-being in this precious life is more important to you than the distractions that fall on you like rain.

"I still get distracted!" Please don't make the mistake of giving up your mindfulness practice just because distraction continues to happen. Defeat mindlessness with a deliberate, grounded practice. Defeat your stable misery with therapeutic doses of healthy choices. Each of the four pillars of well-being build the foundation of the life you seek, one with much less rumination and worry than you engage in now. You must make the right choices to receive your rewards; mindfulness comes to those who sit, not those who run away!

Don't be disheartened if you feel that you keep getting distracted. Distraction is actually the terrain in which mindfulness grows. When you return to mindful awareness from mindless distraction, it's often in coming back to the awareness of your breath—awareness of yourself as a living being—that allows you to feel centered.

This paradoxical relationship between distraction and mindfulness has much larger implications. Mindfulness is the tree from which the fruit of radical acceptance grows. Just as mindfulness and distraction are often interconnected, compassion is often interconnected with the obstacles that challenge you. Mindfulness allows you the opportunity to transform your distractions and obstacles into tools for growth.

Mindfulness teaches your brain how your mind can help you cope and grow with life's various tests. My clinical experiences with cancer patients have taught me that when people are present, or mindful, with more openness and radical acceptance than they previously thought possible, their worst fears and most torturous moments can fuel a relentless quest for a much deeper joy, meaning, and compassion than they previously thought possible. As the old saying goes, "When one door closes, another one opens." Using the mindful path, you can use life's challenges to help you transform into the person you've always wanted to be.

You don't have to wait for a serious illness to train yourself to become resilient. The time for such training is now, in this moment, in this and every day. You don't pack your bags at the airport; you are learning how to come to life's challenges prepared.

"Forgiveness can be really hard!" Another of the hardships practitioners encounter is the challenge of forgiveness. It can sound noble, but it's far from easy. Mindfulness can draw your awareness to your mind's automatic thoughts and feelings, allowing you to take a step back, with radical acceptance, so you can avoid getting consumed by your own self-importance. In the window that mindfulness opens is the potential to forgive yourself and others for past perceived wrongs, and forgive yourself for having made regrettable choices.

You're not required to give up your self-esteem, self-love, or dignity. Instead, you're asked to give up the self-centeredness that can come from spending too much energy focused on your own worries, anxieties, grudges, pain, and suffering. Your self-centeredness and self-importance—not your self-worth—are changed by your heartfelt wish that your adversaries and others be free from suffering, in the same way that you wish to free yourself from suffering. You don't have to forget people's past actions to forgive them for the suffering they brought you. Forgiveness shouldn't be confused with becoming naive. However, forgiveness is balancing unconditional self-love with care for others and the awareness of yourself as just one part of an infinite universe.

Many people find it easier to give up mindfulness practice than to balance their sense of self-importance or to even consider forgiving someone. Even after all these years, it's still sometimes easier for me to hold onto my own self-importance than to automatically forgive.

But mindfulness makes me aware of when I do this, and instead of giving in to guilt, anger, hatred, and resentment for long periods, I feel that I'm much more careful to focus my energy on positive goals. When anger, hatred, and resentment arise, I know they're challenging me to expand my capacity for compassion and radical acceptance. My mind can dance with these disturbing feelings, and sometimes even find comfort in the thoughts and fantasies they bring, but it knows the light of compassion will soon get turned on.

Please don't make the mistake of sacrificing your own dedicated mindfulness practice for the sake of your self-importance.

rewards of the practice

The role of forgiveness is not to be underestimated. In the traditional Buddhist context, greater mindfulness in itself is a goal, but the eventual goal of mindfulness is compassion. Where does compassion lead?

At the very least, you can become a better person. In the Buddhist doctrines, compassion leads to enlightenment, the direct perception of ultimate reality that gives healing, peace, unlimited wisdom, and transcendence. Buddhists believe that upon attaining enlightenment, we can choose to escape from the cycle of birth, old age, sickness, death, and rebirth if we wish to do so. In other traditions, enlightenment is put into the language of being with God, or the creator, in some way. Both types of traditions suggest that enlightenment is piercing the veil of our individual existence and becoming conscious of a vast, cosmic reality.

All wisdom traditions seem to agree on this: love, compassion, and forgiveness are our duties as human beings on earth. The stakes for our individual mental health and the well-being of all life-forms on our planet are too high for them to be subject to our distracted self-importance. The journey to our holistic survival—physical, mental, emotional, spiritual, and environmental—begins and ends with our ability to develop a compassionate love for ourselves that we can spread into the darkest and unlikeliest of places in order to move our lives to a more dignified and healthy place. We're to retell the story of each moment of our lives with unconditional love, mindfulness, and gratitude. Each moment is a step toward our life-long wellness and well-being.

Ironically, the path toward your individual well-being lies in diminishing your sense of self-importance, in letting go of your petty jealousies, resentments, anger, and anxiety to focus instead on your resilience, meaning, and joys.

a call to action

Reading this book and learning about the benefits of mindfulness, exercise, a healthy diet, and good sleep isn't enough. You must put these routines into practice; otherwise you're wasting the precious moments of your life that you could spend in enjoyment, awareness, and happiness. Without your regular, continuous efforts to maintain your healthy choices, every precious moment you spent reading this book was a waste of your time. You won't get those moments back, but you can use them as a springboard to your new life.

1. Begin now with feeling your breath rising and falling in your body.

2. Notice the sensations of your body as you breathe.

3. Bring your awareness to your breath, to your sensations, to your posture.

4. Bringing your mind into this moment is freedom—the freedom to live up to your best potential.

5. It all begins with this moment.

6. With each moment, it begins now.

mindfulness resources

meditation retreat centers

After a while, you may choose to go on a retreat, whether for a few hours or several days, to deepen your practice. If you can't find a local mindfulness retreat center, the following locations host a variety of programs and opportunities to help you grow:

- Esalen Institute, Big Sur, California: www.esalen.org

- Hollyhock, Cortes Island, British Columbia, Canada: www.hollyhock.ca/cms

- Insight Meditation Society, Barre, Massachusetts: www.dharma.org

- Santa Barbara Institute for Consciousness Studies, Santa Barbara, California, and other locations: www.sbinstitute.com

- Spirit Rock Meditation Center, Woodacre, California: www.spiritrock.org

- Upaya Institute and Zen Center, Santa Fe, New Mexico: www.upaya.org

recommended reading

In addition to practice and going on retreat, you may wish to increase your knowledge of mindfulness and meditation by reading the following books, which I've found to be very helpful over the years:

Brach, T. 2004. *Radical Acceptance: Embracing Your Life with the Heart of a Buddha*. New York: Bantam Books.

Chödrön, P. 2005. *When Things Fall Apart: Heart Advice for Difficult Times*. Boston, MA: Shambhala Publications.

Dass, R. 1990. *Journey of Awakening: A Meditator's Guidebook*. New York: Bantam Books.

H.H. Dalai Lama, and H. C. Cutler. 1998. *The Art of Happiness: A Handbook for Living*. New York: Penguin Books.

Kabat-Zinn, J. 2005. *Wherever You Go, There You Are: Mindfulness Meditation in Everyday Life*. New York: Hyperion Books.

Thich Nhat Hanh. 1999. *Miracle of Mindfulness*. Boston, MA: Beacon Press.

Trungpa, C. 2008. *Cutting Through Spiritual Materialism*. Boston, MA: Shambhala Publications.

internet resources

You can find me online at www.twitter.com/sameetkumar and also on my blog, "Mindful Synergy," at http://sameetkumar.blogspot.com. Check back often for updates, information on appearences, and the latest in discoveries related to the mindful path.

You can also read the Buddha's original teachings, translated into English, at www.accesstoinsight.com/tipitaka/index.html.

references

Ackermann, R., and R. J. DeRubeis. 1991. Is depressive realism real? *Clinical Psychology Review* 11 (5):565–84.

Ainsworth, M. D. S., M. C. Blehar, M., E. Waters, and S. Wall. 1978. *Patterns of Attachment: A Psychological Study of the Strange Situation.* Hillsdale, NJ: Lawrence Erlbaum Associates.

Andréasson, A., L. Arborelius, C. Erlanson-Albertsson, and M. Lekander. 2007. A putative role for cytokines in the impaired appetite in depression. *Brain, Behavior, and Immunity* 21 (2):147–52.

Antunes, H. K. M, S. G. Stella, R. F. Santos, O. F. A. Bueno, and M. T. de Mello. 2005. Depression, anxiety, and quality of life scores in seniors after an endurance exercise program. *Revista Brasileira de Psiquiatria* 27 (4):266–71.

Beck, A. T., A. J. Rush, B. F. Shaw, and G. Emery. 1987. *Cognitive Therapy of Depression.* New York: The Guilford Press.

Bowlby, J. 1988. *A Secure Base: Clinical Applications of Attachment Theory.* London: Routledge.

Brenes, G. A., J. D. Williamson, S. P. Messier, W. J. Rejeski, M. Pahor, E. Ip, and B. W. Penninx. 2007. Treatment of minor depression in older adults: A pilot study comparing sertraline and exercise. *Aging and Mental Health* 11 (1):61–68.

Broderick, P. C. 2005. Mindfulness and coping with dysphoric mood: Contrasts with rumination and distraction. *Cognitive Therapy and Research* 29 (5):501–10.

Burnette, J. L., D. E. Davis, J. D. Green, E. L. Worthington Jr., and E. Bradfield. 2009. Insecure attachment and depressive symptoms: The mediating role of rumination, empathy, and forgiveness. *Personality and Individual Differences* 46 (3):276–80.

Carlson, L. E., and S. N. Garland. 2005. Impact of mindfulness-based stress reduction (MBSR) on sleep, mood, stress, and fatigue symptoms in cancer outpatients. *International Journal of Behavioral Medicine* 12 (4):278–85.

Carmody, J., and R. A. Baer. 2008. Relationships between mindfulness practice and levels of mindfulness, medical and psychological symptoms, and well-being in a mindfulness-based stress reduction program. *Journal of Behavioral Medicine* 31 (1):23–33.

Chiron, C., I. Jambaque, R. Nabbout, R. Lounes, A. Syrota, and O. Dulac. 1997. The right brain hemisphere is dominant in human infants. *Brain* 120 (6):1057–65.

Christie, B. R., B. D. Eadie, T. S. Kannangara, J. M. Robillard, J. Shin, and A. K. Titterness. 2008. Exercising our brains: How physical activity impacts synaptic plasticity in the dentate gyrus. *NeuroMolecular Medicine* 10 (2):47–58.

Coffey, K. A., and M. Hartman. 2008. Mechanisms of action in the inverse relationship between mindfulness and psychological distress. *Complementary Health Practice Review* 13 (2):79–91.

Cohen, D. A., and T. A. Farley. 2008. Eating as an automatic behavior. *Preventing Chronic Disease* 5 (1):1–7.

Cotman, C. W., N. C. Berchtold, and L. A. Christie. 2007. Exercise builds brain health: Key roles of growth factor cascades and inflammation. *Trends in Neurosciences* 30 (9):464–72.

Cox, B. J., M. W. Enns, J. R. Walker, K. Kjernisted, and S. R. Pidlubny. 2001. Psychological vulnerabilities in patients with major depression vs. panic disorder. *Behaviour Research and Therapy* 39 (5):567–73.

Creswell, J. D., B. M. Way, N. I. Eisenberger, and M. D. Lieberman. 2007. Neural correlates of dispositional mindfulness during affect labeling. *Psychosomatic Medicine* 69 (6):560–65.

Davidson, R. J., J. Kabat-Zinn, J. Schumacher, M. Rosenkranz, D. Muller, S. F. Santorelli, F. Urbanowski, A. Harrington, K. Bonus, and J. F. Sheridan. 2003. Alterations in brain and immune function produced by mindfulness meditation. *Psychosomatic Medicine* 65 (4):564–70.

Davila, J., and R. J. Cobb. 2003. Predicting change in self-reported and interviewer-assessed adult attachment: Tests of the individual difference and life stress models of attachment change. *Personality and Social Psychology Bulletin* 29 (7):859–70.

di Paula, A., and J. D. Campbell. 2002. Self-esteem and persistence in the face of failure. *Journal of Personality and Social Psychology* 83 (3):711–24.

Drevets, W. C. 2001. Neuroimaging and neuropathological studies of depression: Implications for the cognitive-emotional features of mood disorders. *Current Opinion in Neurobiology* 11 (2):240–49.

Drevets, W. C., J. L. Price, and M. L. Furey. 2008. Brain structural and functional abnormalities in mood disorders: Implications for neurocircuitry models of depression. *Brain Structure and Function* 213 (1–2):93–118.

Duman, R. S. 2005. Neurotrophic factors and regulation of mood: Role of exercise, diet, and metabolism. *Neurobiology of Aging* 26 (Suppl. 1):88–93.

Dunn, A. L., M. H. Trivedi, J. B. Kampert, C. G. Clark, and H. O. Chambliss. 2005. Exercise treatment for depression: Efficacy and dose response. *American Journal of Preventive Medicine* 28 (1):1–8.

Ellenbogen, J. M., P. T. Hu, J. D. Payne, D. Titone, and M. P. Walker. 2007. Human relational memory requires time and sleep. *Proceedings of the National Academy of Sciences* 104 (18):7723–28.

Farb, N. A. S., Z. V. Segal, H. Mayberg, J. Bean, D. McKeon, Z. Fatima, and A. K. Anderson. 2007. Attending to the present: Mindfulness meditation reveals distinct neural modes of self-reference. *Social Cognitive and Affective Neuroscience* 2 (4):313–22.

Frankl, V. E. 2006. *Man's Search for Meaning.* Boston: Beacon Press.

Glicken, M. D. 2006. *Learning from Resilient People: Lessons We Can Apply to Counseling and Psychotherapy.* Thousand Oaks, CA: Sage Publications.

Guastella, A. J., and M. L. Moulds. 2007. The impact of rumination on sleep quality following a stressful life event. *Personality and Individual Differences* 42 (6):1151–62.

Gyatso, T. 2000. *Annutarayoga-tantra ka abhisheka* (Buddhist initiation ceremony), August 10–17, in Ki Gompa, Spiti District, HP, India.

———. 2004. Teachings on "Instructions on the Garland of Views" by Padmasambhava, September 20–21, at University of Miami Convocation Center, Coral Gables, FL.

Haack, M., and J. M. Mullington. 2005. Sustained sleep restriction reduces emotional and physical well-being. *Pain* 119 (1–3):56–64.

Harding, S., and Thrangu Rinpoche. 2002. *Creation and Completion: Essential Points of Tantric Meditation.* Somerville, MA: Wisdom Publications.

Harris, P. W., C. J. Pepper, and D. J. Maack. 2008. The relationship between maladaptive perfectionism and depressive symptoms: The mediating role of rumination. *Personality and Individual Differences* 44 (1):150–60.

Hendrickx, H., B. S. McEwen, and F. van der Ouderaa. 2005. Metabolism, mood, and cognition in aging: The importance of lifestyle and dietary intervention. *Neurobiology of Aging* 26 (Suppl. 1):1–5.

Hölzel, B. K., U. Ott, T. Gard, H. Hempel, M. Weygandt, K. Morgen, and D. Vaitl. 2008. Investigation of mindfulness meditation practitioners with voxel-based morphometry. *Social Cognitive and Affective Neuroscience* 3 (1):55–61.

Kabat-Zinn, J. 1982. An outpatient program in behavioral medicine for chronic pain patients based on the practice of mindfulness meditation: Theoretical considerations and preliminary results. *General Hospital Psychiatry* 4 (1):33–47.

———. 1990. *Full Catastrophe Living: Using the Wisdom of Your Body and Mind to Face Stress, Pain, and Illness.* New York: Dell Publishing.

Kumar, S., G. Feldman, and A. Hayes. 2008. Changes in mindfulness and emotion regulation in an exposure-based cognitive therapy for depression. *Cognitive Therapy and Research* 32 (6):734–44.

Ludwig, D. S., and J. Kabat-Zinn. 2008. Mindfulness in medicine. *Journal of the American Medical Association* 300 (11):1350–52.

Lyubomirsky, S., and S. Nolen-Hoeksema. 1995. Effects of self-focused rumination on negative thinking and interpersonal problem solving. *Journal of Personality and Social Psychology* 69 (1):176–90.

Lyubomirsky, S., K. M. Sheldon, and D. Schkade. 2005. Pursuing happiness: The architecture of sustainable change. *Review of General Psychology* 9 (2):111–31.

McCullough, M. E., C. G. Bellah, S. D. Kilpatrick, and J. L. Johnson. 2001. Vengefulness: Relationships with forgiveness, rumination, well-being, and the big five. *Personality and Social Psychology Bulletin* 27 (5):601–10.

Mickelson, K. D., R. C. Kessler, and P. R. Shaver. 1997. Adult attachment in a nationally representative sample. *Journal of Personality and Social Psychology* 73 (5):1092–1106.

Mikulincer, M., and V. Florian. 1999. The association between parental reports of attachment style and family dynamics, and offspring's reports of adult attachment style. *Family Process* 38 (2):243–57.

Mikulincer, M., P. R. Shaver, O. Gillath, and R. A. Nitzberg. 2005. Attachment, caregiving, and altruism: Boosting attachment security increases compassion and helping. *Journal of Personality and Social Psychology* 89 (5):817–39.

Milner, B., L. R. Squire, and E. R. Kandel. 1998. Cognitive neuroscience and the study of memory. *Neuron* 20 (3):445–68.

Nolen-Hoeksema, S. 2000. The role of rumination in depressive disorders and mixed anxiety/depressive symptoms. *Journal of Abnormal Psychology* 109 (3):504–11.

Nolen-Hoeksema, S., J. Larson, and C. Grayson. 1999. Explaining the gender difference in depressive symptoms. *Journal of Personality and Social Psychology* 77 (5):1061–72.

Palmer, M., E. Breuilly, C. Wai Ming, and J. Ramsay, trans. 2006. *The Book of Chuang Tzu.* New York: Penguin Books.

Schore, A. N. 2001. The effects of a secure attachment relationship on right brain development, affect regulation, and infant mental health. *Infant Mental Health Journal* 22:7–66.

Shantideva. 1992. *A Guide to the Bodhisattva's Way of Life.* Trans. S. Batchelor. Dharamsala, India: Library of Tibetan Works and Archives.

Shaver, P. R., and M. Mikulincer. 2008. Adult attachment and cognitive and affective reactions to positive and negative events. *Social and Personality Psychology Compass* 2 (5):1844–65.

Siegel, D. J. 2001. Toward an interpersonal neurobiology of the developing mind: Attachment relationships, "mindsight," and neural integration. *Infant Mental Health Journal* 22 (1–2):67–94.

Siegel, D. J., and M. Hartzell. 2003. *Parenting from the Inside Out: How a Deeper Self-Understanding Can Help You Raise Children Who Thrive.* New York: Penguin Books.

Speca, M., L. E. Carlson, E. Goodey, and M. Angen. 2000. A randomized, wait-list controlled clinical trial: The effect of a mindfulness meditation-based stress reduction program on mood and symptoms of stress in cancer outpatients. *Psychosomatic Medicine* 62 (5):613–22.

Taylor, S. E., and J. D. Brown. 1994. Positive illusions and well-being revisited: Separating fact from fiction. *Psychological Bulletin* 116 (1):21–27.

Taylor, S. E., M. E. Kemeny, G. M. Reed, J. E. Bower, and T. L. Gruenewald. 2000. Psychological resources, positive illusions, and health. *American Psychologist* 55 (1):99–109.

Teasdale, J. D., Z. V. Segal, J. M. Williams, V. A. Ridgeway, J. M. Soulsby, and M. A. Lau. 2000. Prevention of relapse/recurrence in major depression by mindfulness-based cognitive therapy. *Journal of Consulting and Clinical Psychology* 68 (4):615–23.

Thanissaro Bhikkhu, trans. 2007. Samyutta Nikaya, *Chiggala Sutta* 56:48. www.accesstoinsight.org/tipitaka/sn/sn56/sn56.048.than. html (accessed May 26, 2009).

Treynor, W., R. Gonzalez, and S. Nolen-Hoeksema. 2003. Rumination reconsidered: A psychometric analysis. *Cognitive Therapy and Research* 27 (3):247–59.

Vassilopoulos, S. P. 2008. Social anxiety and ruminative self-focus. *Journal of Anxiety Disorders* 22 (5):860–67.

Vitetta, L., B. Anton, F. Cortizo, and A. Sali. 2005. Mind-body medicine: Stress and its impact on overall health and longevity. *Annals of the New York Academy of Sciences* 1057:492–505.

Walshe, M., trans. 1987. *Thus Have I Heard: The Long Discourses of the Buddha.* London: Wisdom Publications.

Waters, E., S. Merrick, D. Treboux, J. Crowell, and L. Albersheim. 2000. Attachment security in infancy and early adulthood: A twenty-year longitudinal study. *Child Development* 71 (3):684–89.

Wegner, D. M., D. J. Schneider, S. R. Carter III, and T. L. White. 1987. Paradoxical effects of thought suppression. *Journal of Personality and Social Psychology* 53 (1):5–13.

Wei, M., P. P. Heppner, and B. Mallinckrodt. 2003. Perceived coping as a mediator between attachment and psychological distress: A structural equation modeling approach. *Journal of Counseling Psychology* 50 (4):438–47.

Sameet M. Kumar, Ph.D., is a Buddhist psychotherapist who works at the Memorial Cancer Institute of the Memorial Healthcare System in Broward County, FL. His areas of expertise include mindfulness-based therapies, palliative care, spirituality in psychotherapy, stress management and relaxation, and grief and bereavement. He has trained with many leading Hindu and Tibetan Buddhist teachers and has traveled extensively in India, China, and Tibet. Read his blog at sameetkumar.blogspot.com and get regular updates at twitter.com/sameetkumar.

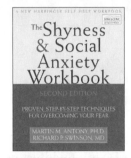